I. THE WORDS OF THE GOSPELS

SAINT MATTHEW

JACOB begat Joseph, the husband of Mary, of whom was born Jesus who is called Christ.

Now the birth of Jesus Christ was on this wise: When as his mother Mary was espoused to Joseph, before they came together, she was found with child of the Holy Ghost. Then Joseph her husband, being a just man, and not willing to make her a publick example, was minded to put her away privily. But while he thought on these things, behold, an angel of the Lord appeared unto him in a dream, saying, Joseph, thou son of David, fear not to take unto thee Mary thy wife: for that which is conceived in her is of the Holy Ghost. And she shall bring forth a son, and thou shalt call his name Jesus: for he shall save his people from their sins. Now all this was done that it might be fulfilled which was spoken of the Lord by the prophet, saying, Behold a virgin shall conceive and bear a son, and they shall call his name Emmanuel, which, being interpreted, is, God with us. Then Joseph, being raised from sleep, did as the angel of the Lord had bidden him, and took unto him his wife: and knew her not until she had brought forth her first-born son: and he called his name Jesus.

When [the wise men] were come into the house, they saw the young child with Mary his mother, and fell down and worshipped him.

And when they were departed, behold, the angel of the Lord appeared to Joseph in a dream, saying, Arise and take the young child and his mother, and flee into Egypt, and be thou there until I bring thee word: for Herod will seek the

B   I

young child to destroy him. And he arose, and took the young child and his mother by night, and departed into Egypt.

When Herod was dead, behold an angel of the Lord appeareth in a dream to Joseph in Egypt, saying, Arise and take the young child and his mother, and go into the land of Israel: for they are dead that sought the young child's life. And he arose and took the young child and his mother, and came into the land of Israel.

While [Jesus] yet talked to the people, behold his mother and his brethren stood without, desiring to speak with him. Then one said unto him, Behold, thy mother and thy brethren stand without, desiring to speak with thee. But he answered and said unto him that told him, Who is my mother, and who are my brethren? And he stretched forth his hand toward his disciples, and said, Behold my mother and my brethren. For whosoever shall do the will of my Father which is in Heaven, the same is my brother, and sister, and mother.

SAINT MARK

THERE came then his brethren and his mother, and, standing without, sent unto him, calling him. And the multitude sat about him, and they said unto him, Behold thy mother and thy brethren without seek for thee. And he answered them, saying, Who is my mother, or my brethren? And he looked round about on them which sat about him, and said, Behold my mother and my brethren. For whosoever shall do the will of God, the same is my brother, and my sister, and my mother.

SAINT LUKE

THE angel Gabriel was sent from God unto a city of Galilee named Nazareth, to a virgin espoused to a man whose name was Joseph, of the house of David; and the virgin's name was Mary. And the angel came in unto her, and said, Hail, thou that art highly favoured, the Lord is with thee: blessed

Mary the Mother of Jesus

MARY

THE MOTHER OF JESUS

by

Alice Meynell

With eight plates in colour after
R. Anning Bell, R.A.

LONDON

The MEDICI SOCIETY *Limited*

SEVEN GRAFTON STREET, also at BOSTON, U.S.A.

LIVERPOOL, 63 BOLD ST, & 121 OLD CHRISTCHURCH RD., BOURNEMOUTH

First published 1912
New Edition *October,* 1923

PRINTED IN GREAT BRITAIN

ৰ CONTENTS ৰ

ৰ A LIST OF THE PLATES ৰ

art thou among women. And when she saw him, she was troubled at his saying, and cast in her mind what manner of salutation this should be. And the angel said unto her, Fear not, Mary, for thou hast found favour with God. And, behold, thou shalt conceive in thy womb, and bring forth a son, and shalt call his name Jesus. He shall be great, and shall be called the son of the Highest: and the Lord God shall give unto him the throne of his father David; and he shall reign over the house of Jacob for ever; and of his kingdom there shall be no end. Then said Mary unto the angel, How shall this be, seeing I know not a man? And the angel answered and said unto her, The Holy Ghost shall come upon thee, and the power of the Highest shall overshadow thee; therefore also that holy thing which shall be born of thee shall be called the Son of God. And behold thy cousin Elizabeth, she hath also conceived a son in her old age: and this is the sixth month with her who was called barren. For with God nothing shall be impossible. And Mary said, Behold the handmaid of the Lord; be it unto me according to thy word. And the angel departed from her.

And Mary arose in those days, and went into the hill country with haste, into a city of Juda, and entered into the house of Zacharias, and saluted Elizabeth. And it came to pass that when Elizabeth heard the salutation of Mary, the babe leaped in her womb; and Elizabeth was filled with the Holy Ghost. And she spake out with a loud voice, and said, Blessed art thou among women, and blessed is the fruit of thy womb. And whence is this to me, that the mother of my Lord should come to me? For lo, as soon as the voice of thy salutation sounded in mine ears, the babe leaped in my womb for joy. And blessed is she that believed; for there shall be a performance of those things which were told her from the Lord.

And Mary said, My soul doth magnify the Lord, and my spirit hath rejoiced in God my Saviour. For he hath regarded the low estate of his handmaiden; for behold, from henceforth all generations shall call me blessed. For he that is mighty hath done to me great things, and holy is his name. And his mercy is on them that fear him, from generation to generation. He hath shewed strength with his arm; he hath scattered the proud in the imagination of their hearts. He hath put down the mighty from their seats, and exalted them of low degree. He hath filled the hungry with good things, and the rich he hath sent empty away. He hath holpen his servant Israel in remembrance of his mercy; as he spake to our fathers, to Abraham, and to his seed for ever.

And Mary abode with her about three months, and returned to her own house.

And Joseph went up from Galilee, out of the city of Nazareth, into Judæa, unto the city of David, which is called Bethlehem, . . . to be taxed, with Mary his espoused wife, being great with child. And so it was that while they were there, the days were accomplished that she should be delivered. And she brought forth her first-born son, and wrapped him in swaddling clothes, and laid him in a manger; because there was no room for them in the inn.

And there were in the same country shepherds abiding in the field, keeping watch over their flock by night. And lo, the angel of the Lord came upon them, and the glory of the Lord shone round about them ; and they were sore afraid. And the angel said unto them, Fear not; for behold I bring you good tidings ot great joy, which shall be to all people. For unto you is born this day in the city of David a Saviour, which is Christ the Lord. And this shall be a sign unto you: Ye shall find the babe wrapped in swaddling clothes, lying in a manger. And suddenly there was with the angel a multitude of the heavenly host praising God and saying, Glory to God in the highest, and on earth peace, good will toward men.[1]

---

[1] *Greek,* Peace to men of good pleasure. *Douai translation,* Peace to men of good will.

And it came to pass, as the angels were gone away from them into heaven, the shepherds said one to another, Let us now go even unto Bethlehem, and see this thing which is come to pass, which the Lord hath made known unto us. And they came with haste, and found Mary, and Joseph, and the babe lying in a manger. And when they had seen it, they made known abroad the saying which was told them concerning the child. And all they that heard it wondered at those things which were told them by the shepherds.

But Mary kept all these things, and pondered them in her heart.

And when the days of her purification according to the law of Moses were accomplished, they brought him to Jerusalem, to present him to the Lord. . . . And Joseph and his mother marvelled at those things which were spoken of him. And Simeon blessed them, and said unto Mary his mother, Behold this child is set for the fall and rising again of many in Israel, and for a sign that shall be spoken against ; (Yea, and a sword shall pierce through thy own soul also,) that the thoughts of many hearts may be revealed.

And when they had performed all things according to the law of the Lord, they returned into Galilee, to their own city Nazareth. And the child grew, and waxed strong in spirit, filled with wisdom; and the grace of God was upon him.

Now his parents went to Jerusalem every year at the feast of the passover. And when he was twelve years old, they went up to Jerusalem after the custom of the feast. And when they had fulfilled the days, as they returned, the child Jesus tarried behind in Jerusalem ; and Joseph and his mother knew not of it. But they, supposing him to have been in the company, went a day's journey ; and they sought him among their kinsfolk and acquaintance. And when they found him not, they turned back again to Jerusalem, seeking him. And it came to pass that after three days they found him in the temple, sitting in the midst of the doctors, both hearing them and asking them questions. And all that heard him were astonished at his understanding and answers. And when they saw him they were amazed: and his mother said unto him, Son, why hast thou thus dealt with us? Behold, thy father and I have sought thee sorrowing. And he said unto them, How is it that ye sought me? Wist ye not that I must be about my father's business? And they understood not the saying which he spake unto them. And he went down with them, and came to Nazareth, and was subject unto them : but his mother kept all these sayings in her heart.

And Jesus increased in wisdom and stature, and in favour with God and man.

Then came to him his mother and his brethren, and could not come at him for the press. And it was told him by certain which said, Thy mother and thy brethren stand without, desiring to see thee. And he answered and said unto them, My mother and my brethren are these which hear the word of God and do it.

SAINT JOHN

THERE was a marriage in Cana of Galilee ; and the mother of Jesus was there. And both Jesus was called, and his disciples to the marriage. And when they wanted wine, the mother of Jesus saith unto him, They have no wine. Jesus saith unto her, Woman, what have I to do with thee? [1] Mine hour is not yet come. His mother saith unto

---

[1] *Douai translation*, Woman, what is it to me and to thee?

Robert Stephen Hawker, Vicar of Morwenstow, has this note to the name or title Aishah (translated Woman in the English Testament): " The household word for the sinless Mother in the cottage of Nazareth and on the lips of her Son, was Aishah . . . It was not, in that language, a mere appellation of sex

the servants, Whatsoever he saith unto you, do it. And there were set there six waterpots of stone, after the manner of the purifying of the Jews, containing two or three firkins apiece. Jesus saith unto them, Fill the waterpots with water. And they filled them up to the brim. And he saith unto them, Draw out now, and bear unto the governor of the feast. And they bare it. When the ruler of the feast had tasted the water that was made wine, and knew not whence it was, (but the servants which drew the water knew,) the governor of the feast called the bridegroom, and saith unto him, Every man at the beginning doth set forth good wine ; and when men have well drunk, then that which is worse; but thou hast kept the good wine until now.

This beginning of miracles did Jesus in Cana of Galilee, and manifested forth his glory; and his disciples believed on him. After this he went down to Capernaum, he, and his mother, and his brethren, and his disciples.

Now there stood by the cross of Jesus his mother, and his mother's sister, Mary the wife of Cleophas, and Mary Magdalene. When Jesus therefore saw his mother, and the disciple standing by whom he loved, he saith unto his mother, Woman, behold thy son. Then saith he to the disciple, Behold thy mother. And from that hour that disciple took her unto his own home.

THE ACTS OF THE APOSTLES
THESE [disciples] all continued with one accord in prayer and supplication, with the women, and Mary the mother of Jesus, and with his brethren.

—Woman—but Aishah, the tender and graceful title . . . At the marriage, when, with her woman's zeal for the honour of the feast, the Mother made haste to her Son, and said suddenly, They have no wine, . . . He said in the exact letter, What is it to me and to thee, Aishah?"

II. MARY IN THE SCRIPTURES

THE theology of the older Church does not restrict the life and history and legend of Mary to the New Testament. ·It refers to the Prophets before, and to tradition after, her brief record in the Gospels. Chief of all prophecies is that of Isaiah: "Therefore the Lord Himself shall give you a sign. Behold a Virgin shall conceive and bear a Son and shall call His name Emmanuel (God with us)." In spite of the paraphrase of Matthew Arnold, this form of the words keeps its place in the churches at Christmas; nor will his nineteenth-century English fit the music of Handel who wrote his recitative for English of the sixteenth. Another prophecy, but one much less generally known out of the city of Rome, is inscribed on the pedestal of a modern monument to the honour of Mary, herself the tabernacle of the Son of God. It is a phrase from the book of Exodus, interpreted symbolically: "I will sanctify my Tabernacle."

Saint Luke and Saint John are the two Evangelists to whom the Mother of Our Lord must have entrusted the things she had kept for half an age in her heart. Or rather, her story was told chiefly to Saint Luke, whereas Saint John records those passages of the Passion of Christ of which he was witness at her side: "Now there stood by the Cross of Jesus His mother"; and the Words from the Cross, "Behold thy mother," and "Woman, behold thy son." Saint John took her from that place of sorrows to his own home; with him she joined the Congregation of Apostles at prayer before Pentecost; and in his care she must have "undergone the ceremony of death." Moreover it had been he who put upon eternal record the first miracle worked by Christ, at the prayer of His mother, at Cana of Galilee. But to Saint Luke she dictated the mystery of the Annunciation, and that of the Visitation, and the text of the " Magnificat Anima mea Dominum." The Presentation in the Temple and the Finding in the Temple are mysteries of the Childhood of Christ assigned to Saint Luke alone for record. There is no Annunciation to the Virgin in any other Gospel. In Saint Matthew's Gospel it is made not to her but to Saint Joseph. Saint Luke and Saint Matthew share together the history of the Nativity, for the other two Evangelists begin no earlier than the day of Christ's baptism and His Ministry. The name of Mary is not named by Saint Mark. And in not one of the Gospels of Saint Matthew, Saint Mark, and Saint Luke, is the presence of the Mother at the Crucifixion recorded.

To one modest mind, to one retentive heart, therefore, until the long days in the house of John, were committed, for the years of a man's life, the message of Gabriel; the salutation of the young mother to the aged mother, when two women, alone in the hill-country, carried the destinies of the world; the prophecy of Simeon, the foreknowledge of the sword that should pierce the soul of Mary also, the title of the Mother of Sorrows which that wound should earn for her, and which the thousand thousand daughters of sorrow should invoke in the future world; and how much of that future we cannot conjecture. But we know there was a cluster of august secrets in one maid's heart.

So much, and so little, is told us by her friends, her sons the Evangelists, the companions of her life. The chapter " Mary in the Scriptures " cannot but be one of the shortest. We, in the modern world, which has grown so sensitive— more consciously sensitive, or rather more fastidious, than the world of the Middle Ages—may wish that the silences of the Gospel had never been broken, its great gaps of time never filled, and all that they imply never explained. A sense of art mixes with our modern piety. We are apt to

c

admire the evangelical reticence for its dignity, as we admire, in this passage, what Dante does not tell, and in that, the sudden detail that carves his narrative like a blade. Such details are these:—the interruption that weeping imposes on Francesca, and the poet's swoon, when the whole business and pageant of Hell are suspended and the reader enters for some unknown time into a relief like that of chloroform after intolerable pain ; or the centaur's putting aside of his beard so that he may call audibly in the infernal gale. In like manner we are apt to respect the Scripture narratives with their few intense details, their close events and their great omissions alike, for their simplicity, and—it is to be feared that our literature leads us so far—for their " effect."

But the great Dark Ages were obviously not literary, and the great Middle Ages were literary in another sense than ours. In what the Gospels tell, those centuries found the events upon which they might turn the mind's eyes, never wearied ; and in the silent spaces of the Scriptures they found ample room for meditation. The Christian art of symbolism grew up in that time, when the Bible was virtually the one only book,—read, and read alone, by the few who could read, told to the many who could not, but who could look and who could listen. In both those classes, within the Monastery and in the little town, were childish minds, such as will not be satisfied with a story divided by pauses. " What are they saying ? " asks the child who has been answered as to what the figures in a picture are doing. The keen questioners of the mediæval world would have an answer, as to the parentage and the childhood of Mary, as to her education, as to her espousals and the history of her spouse, as to the childhood of her Son, as to the after history of " the man raised up by Christ," and of his sisters Mary and Martha, as to the identity of Mary Magdalen, as to the names of the bridegroom and bride of Cana of Galilee. Not a nook, not a corner, was to be left unsearched by the urgent questioners for whom the Gospels contained the one

THE ANNUNCIATION

"Hail, thou that art highly favoured, the Lord is with
thee : blessed art thou among women " (*Luke I,* 28)

story most worth hearing. The search became an exploration, and at last a ransacking. To the chief questions the great traditions gave the chief answers; the traditions were living history, having all the immediate vivacity of good news, history conveyed by vital voice to vital voice, history told to children and to their children, and therefore immemorial age by age, history full of pulses that were full of life, history that had never lapsed, and had never held its tongue in a book, history that had made pictures for childlike imaginations in adult grave heads for a thousand years. Such was Tradition in those days, and Tradition was, as it were, enclosed within the boundaries of the written Gospels. But within those boundaries it was all-active.

Soon upon authoritative Tradition followed eager fancy, urgent conjecture. Nothing was to be suffered to escape. Scrutiny came home with triumphs, such as : Well, and who do you think it was who was married when the wine ran short? Who but Saint John, the beloved Disciple, and he and his bride parted at the church door so that they might more closely follow Christ. And who was she? Why, Mary the sister of Lazarus—no other! The popular passion for identifications, for lessening the numbers of the actors in any history, for heaping upon one figure that which befell many, for concentrating, for knotting together, for centralizing—a popular passion that may be noted whenever a hero is hero enough to the people to become the subject of their own song and their own story—this passion was delighted by all the later legends, gathered into the enclosure of the Scriptures. The great power of imagination and the little power of ingenuity alike found matter there; and we cannot wonder that the officious power of invention also went to work.

After the smoke of the destruction and the dust of the demolition of the Empire of Rome had passed and left the air fit for men to breathe—and those clouds hung low and long—Romance, the freshest of all the many beginnings of human history, the freshest, the sweetest, and the most

innocent, had its happy origins. Stories of dragons that are
somewhat too wild for our children were the love-stories of
men and women, and romantic love was born in Europe, and
chastity was at its heart. Adventure led to the Holy Land,
and the goal of all enterprise was the Grave in which the
Gospel closes, the one only forsaken grave in the world, the
grave which the earth with its million million lives carries
round the sun as the chief earthly treasure. Adventure and
love and purity of heart were bound together. For the virtue
dearest to the heart of Romance, dearer than all invention,
all device, all loyalty, all battle, dearer than courage itself,
was the virtue of men, the virtue of soldiers, lovers, and friars
—chastity—dearer chiefly in those regiments, in those camps,
in those castles, and in those cloisters because it was the
virtue of the Virgin of the Gospel. Where else did the
Middle Ages learn it? Assuredly not in the Old Testament,
where the inviolability of the Jewess for a lover of another
race, and of the wife for the sake of the husband's honour,
seem to take its place; where the daughter of Jephtha, before
her early death, went bewailing the virginity that was to
be the very treasure of many thousand cloisters. Not in the
Old Testament do we find the camp raising a choral song in
its honour. Mary in the Gospels set the new example. Across
the reigns of Tiberius, Nero, Elagabalus, and the rest of the
last corruption of Antiquity, that new virtue reached to the
Middle Ages and instituted the ethics, the courts, and the
laws of romantic love. Love came to life with it, as love
will live as long as it endures, and no longer.

III. THE VIRGIN

HE would be but writing admitted history, and making a plain record of what has indubitably been, who should show us the one most important of all our race to have been a woman and a young maid. To say so much is not to impugn the humanity of Christ. We may set Him apart; as man indeed, but not as what the habits of our language would name "a man." His mother, on the contrary, is not only woman, but "a woman"; young, moreover, in the chief time of her office, and held to have been fitted for that office by one only quality—innocence.

If Buddha has been dominant over greater numbers, and Mahomet has kept a longer immediate hold upon great races, Mary has presided over the countries and the people that were most important, that were at work, at war, at thought, and not only or even chiefly at thought or only or chiefly at war. Greatly important men, dominating by decisive battles and by codes of law, have made centralizing eddies in the vitality of the world, but the woman was in truth central. She alone was the ideal human being of dominant races in their most momentous times. To her were attributed the qualities of best report in civilizing ages—and what were these? They were qualities directed, lifted, altered, modified, limited, hampered if you will, by the womanhood, the simplicity, the ignorance, and the weakness of that ideal figure.

In this manner the ideal figure—the all-admired—both shaped, and was shaped by, the aspirations of the world after the passing away of the dominance of Greece, and at the passing away of the dominance of Rome. What this meant in Europe—the head and heart of the world—cannot be measured by the mind of the historian.

The fierce ages and the passionate, the cruel ages during which man starved man to death and man put out the eyes of man for vengeance, were governed by the little Virgin who stood for compassion and innocence, but for innocence before all else. That truth presents an obvious paradox. But other ages show us no less a paradox. Our own, for example, has perhaps more reverence for intellect than for any other human power, but that which draws a million men and women together every night of the revolving year is the imbecility of the music-hall song. Yet none the less assuredly the love of innocence wrought then, as the respect for intellect works now.

To this central human innocence the civilization of the shattered world, re-shaping itself in the great " Dark Ages," was dedicated. To the mind of the world, as it is now, it must seem that no more incredible fact than this has been recorded of our race. It is not that the moral idea is now perilously near to ruin; an attack—an undermine—has indeed been made in our day· the first undermine attempted in the modern world, a plot that shows the old batteries upon structure above-ground to have been comparatively trivial—negligible buttings against the less weighty matters of the law. But in spite of this new fundamental attack, Morality stands. It stands; and, if we imagine it to be figured or symbolized as a person, it stands to-day as a man of early middle age, of the " prime of life," holding his own.

The mediæval centuries, recognizing a Man of early middle age and of the prime of heavenly and earthly life as the Creator of the symbol, did in fact personate morality as a girl, and the simplest of all simple girls. Furthermore, the mediæval mind set back and back the age of the little girl. The mature maid suggested by the Gospel, a young woman about to be married, acquainted with human life, becomes younger and younger in legend and tradition. In painting, indeed, she is mostly a woman of grave years—and the discrepancy is not easily explained—but her legend is

THE VIRGIN AND CHILD, WITH SS. JOHN, ELIZABETH,
JOSEPH, AND SIMEON

" And the child grew, and waxed strong in

the legend of no more than a child. So lasting has been that legend that a Catholic priest preaching, not in Italy where tradition is alive and growing from generation to generation, but in England, has been heard to insist upon Mary's childishness: "A little girl of thirteen!" he cried, as another appeal to his hearers' tenderness and wonder.

That figure presided over the imagination of Europe until the days of the later Renascence. By degrees it withdrew from literature; by swifter degrees in England. One of the later worthy acts of homage in English literature to this ideal innocence is John Evelyn's exquisite "Life of Mrs. Godolphin." Her innocence is there, as Rossetti said of Mary's, "circumspect." Something remains with Richardson and even with Fielding, but a transfiguring beauty had vanished. That former passionate love of innocence has reappeared in the world only in the love of children, of which it has lately boasted perhaps too loudly. But with what a difference has that boast been uttered! And that difference shows more clearly the more we gather together the likenesses of the present admiration with the admiration of the past—that of the little household child, English, French, and American, and that of the little household child Mary.

For instance, take the Doctors and their books. Round about the central Maid of the Middle Ages stand "the judicial Senate of Apostles," the Doctors with their open books, in consultation. They are Doctors of the Church, Latin and Greek; theirs is the highest learning of their time; theirs the noblest intellect; theirs are vigils, theirs are experiences; theirs, in the case of the Latins, is the great language, not old as was thought, but young; to be despised later, in the time of the Renascence, perhaps despised even now; the language that had ceased to be classical, because the classical world was dead, yet the language was not dead but was needed for new meanings, and strong enough to increase, and to carry them—in a word, Christian Latin. It is assuredly an august company; the men are bearded men, "the bearded

counsellors of God"; they are mitred and hold croziers in
their benedictory hands; their eyes are on the open book of
magnificent manuscript or raised as high as the footstool of
the girl about whose character, whose privilege, and whose
office they are there to read and reason. It is upon her innocence that their mind, the chief mind of the re-beginning
world, is bent. There is nothing known to them too grave
or great to be thought, read, or written of her, because she
is innocent. A whole theology is gathered together to assert
her to be innocent in a degree unparalleled and in a manner
unique.

Book in hand, too, note-book in hand, about the child of
our present families stand men of our time, and many of
them are doctors, even though they do not claim the capital
initial; and women, especially in America, have seconded
their studies of their children by keeping note-books of their
own, with dates, doings, and sayings in order. Love there is
in these studies, and a sort of worship of reality; but not a
majestic honour offered to moral perfection in humanity, to
an ideal answered, to the cause and the effect of all possible
human hope. Coldly, or tenderly, or sorrowfully, or quite
impartially, the doctors and the women-saints of this newer
church watch the intelligence and the sweetness, and also
the naughtinesses, the eager grasp and the greed, the stealth
and the cunning, of their little virgins in the family.

Or let the time of life be advanced; and, in the American
fiction of thirty or forty years ago, we find some charming
literature devoted to the young girl. Mr. Howells and
Mr. Henry James, and many writers of less renown, especially the authors of village stories, did honour to what was
then the delicate spirit of American fiction by making the
centre of every novel a self-respecting unmarried woman.
Their young damsel was not august, not noble, not a great
inspirer, but homage to her kept the manners of fiction
singularly incorrupt; yet even then we might wonder a little
to see men who might be bearded, albeit not immediate

"bearded counsellers of God," so closely occupied with her dresses and with the hesitations of her heart in regard to the English peer. Mr. Henry James showed himself later to be made of sterner stuff; but the novelists of that lately past fashion may be pictured in a *sacra conversazione* of their own, unmitred it is true, but also consulting books. The two schools of students are intent, with certain degrees of intentness; these—the mediæval prelates—bent upon magnificent manuscripts (with clasps); those—the present doctors—upon note-books; those again—the novelists—upon little novels. It is true that we need but to gather the likenesses of these various groups in order to see the full measure of their difference. The American girl was called, in her day, the queen of society. We have, then, the queen of the nursery, the queen of society, and the Queen of Heaven, presiding over their respective students and holding their respective courts.

The dominance of an ideal young Maid over the grave intellects and the ardent hearts of the Dark Ages and the Middle Ages has hardly been realized by writers and readers of history, for this paradoxical reason—its signs are too constantly before our eyes. We have "Our Lady" and "By Our Lady" in our Scott, and the Virgin and Child of all the schools of painting. These have become too much a matter of course in our sight to convince us of the prodigy which indeed they imply. Nevertheless it is precisely in a picture gallery that the sight of the truth might take us by surprise. We take the Virgin and Child, the Nativity, the Annunciation, or, say, a martyrdom of St. Lucy, or Angels dancing in a round, all for granted. But we may not have acknowledged the obvious truth—that everything in room after room in all the museums of Europe has been painted in honour of chastity, of humility, of constancy, of self-denial and self-sacrifice, of compassion, of truth, of all that the race of man calls virtue. The masters of the early schools would certainly not easily pardon the modern man who should explain them to his own times as painters who cared nothing for the matter of their picture and only for the manner. But supposing that their Holy Families and the rest were a convention, and that the painters did work for hire from the monasteries, with all the remarks and reflections upon that fact to be found in books—none the less is a convention brought about by a great agreement; and the monasteries were not there by accident. The museum, at any rate, shows one convention, and the yearly exhibition of our present customs another; such another that it has become almost incredible—albeit it is visibly certain—that for certain centuries of the history of European nations art was almost entirely devoted to all the virtues, and all the virtues centred about a girl.

How is it that the contrast, on this one point, between the Dark and Middle Ages and our Lightsome and Final Ages does not daily—in that one region of the picture galleries— amaze us? It is as easily conceivable that the London and Paris of the twentieth century should fill their theatres with audiences assembled to see plays ending with Heaven for the just and Hell for the unjust, or that their citizens should obey St. James in the music-halls—"Is any man merry? let him sing psalms"—as that the "studios" should be dedicated, as the "workshops" were, to the visible images of sanctity and simplicity; to the triumphs of the Martyrs too, to the theology of the Doctors, but above all, enthroned above all, to the mere innocence of a Maid.

IV. THE MOTHER

THE meditations of the many centuries of Christian devotion have pored upon those vacant spaces of the Biblical history where Mary of Nazareth stands, or rather is hidden, as the mother of a Child, of a Boy, of a young Man living at home in a village. Mother, foster-father, and Child are shown to us in Scripture for a few days or hours out of many years: at the Nativity; at the Epiphany ; in Egypt; then twelve years after the Nativity, some score of years before the Mission, in Jerusalem. Here at last Christ speaks. Joseph and Mary had retraced anxious steps in search of Him, meeting their kinsfolk group by group, returning whence they came, to the spring and source of the stream, the fountain of the national life, to the mysterious Temple that was the symbol of the Body of their Son. The few words spoken within the group of three, so often called the earthly Trinity—man, woman, and child—the question and answer, are set down, and no more. These are preserved for us of all the questions and answers of the life in the narrow house. We may suppose that the publicity of this manifestation of the growing Boy—the first manifestation since the Epiphany—suggested the public record of the Gospel, the daily words and daily actions remaining a confidence, or even a secret, of the house. Or we may suppose the daily conversation, never less than holy, to have been always less than prophetic, and the words in the Temple to have been kept in Mary's heart as a great exception, a surprise, an omen, a menace, and a promise.

However this may be, in that maternal heart lay the Gospel of the youth of Christ. Before the pens of the four greatest writers of the world had been set to their task, the New Testament lurked in one woman's memory and in her watchfulness. It was her work to choose and to reject what should be said. Tradition may have preserved something credible, we are free to think so or not; but for what the Scriptures tell we have her word who was for a time herself the New Testament and the Church—a Testament sealed, and a Church expectant, not yet suffering, not yet militant, and not yet triumphant, and only the continent of hope.

The Religious Orders of the older Church divided amongst themselves the several mysteries of the Maternity of Mary— "joyful," "sorrowful," and "glorious." And the joy, the sorrow, and the glory are alike reflected. Christ's was the Passion, but His mother's only the Compassion. The mothers of all ages are those who have suffered because others suffered; for each of them, self is less sensitive than the self of her child. Self is not locked up in the maternal heart, there to be cherished, as it is by the egoist, or to be crushed and silenced as it is by the Saint. In the mother, self is not lost, but loses all its evil by the passionate personal love that distributes it among sons and daughters. Perfect self-less love would perhaps be distributed through the multitude, but a mother is not perfect; nature has so much use for her—separate, family use—that she cannot let her go free from irrational, indispensable partialities and limitings, even injustices, all serving the turn of the race. And these very injustices have so delighted mankind that Thackeray, for instance, makes a heroine of her who will not only defame herself by denying her own legal marriage, but will by the same act defraud the lawful heirs to certain possessions so that the foster-child she loves may enjoy them. This is surely the corruption of a fine thing humanly incomplete. For a mother's partial love that merits any of the reverence, or worthily calls up any of the wonder, of the contemplative man or novelist is not so much unjust as merely incomplete. Incomplete in regard to the extent of

"BUT MARY KEPT ALL THESE THINGS, AND PONDERED THEM IN HER HEART"

(Luke II, 19)

the world and human kind, not incomplete in time; for it passes to a daughter and to a daughter's daughter, to a son and a son's child, and knows no stop in its bequest, and no stop in its consciousness but that of the separation of the grave. Thus finally are bound together the generations, (to use Abigail's words) the bundle of the living.

The admiration of a mother's love has been carried out of bounds in our days, and English writers have taken pains to insist upon its English form. They seem to admire it chiefly as "instinctive," or so one gathers from the novelists. Filial love is most simple in French literature; and most reticent (the reticence is a matter of national self-approval) in our own. Our days are humorous days, and a very great English novelist has bantered the conventional Frenchman's appeal to his mother's memory and to the sanction of her honoured head, her knee at which he was taught, and her grave where his wreath still hangs. This was done humorously by changing the word "mother" to "mama." Filial piety is various in attitude and utterance; and those who have not uttered it at all after their childhood was over have been known to wish that they had given it some speech while the ears to hear it could still hear.

When John Evelyn wishes to praise a contemporary lady by comparing her (to their disadvantage) with illustrious ladies of the past, and especially, as became a scholar and a gentleman, with those of Antiquity, he gives them their titles of honour chiefly as the mothers of the great, and even, in one case, as the mother-in-law. The glory he attributes to these distinguished ladies is a glory reflective and retrospective. In giving them thus a derivative honour he does but rehearse a fact much beyond his present purpose. For the greatest honour ever given to a woman, or indeed to any creature, was absolutely a reflective honour. Of all reflective glory the glory of the Mother of Christ is the supreme example—so perfect an example that it might rather be

called the solitary pattern. Have some enthusiasts seemed
—whether they were poets writing sonnets in honour of the
moon or Christians singing hymns in honour of Mary—to
give their more sensible tenderness to the secondary splendour, have they seemed to forget that the moonlight is the
sunlight simply returned, and Mary a moon to the sun of
Christ, they have only seemed. The consciousness of God as
the giver, the giver of all, lay immovably deep in the heart of
the peasant saying ten " Aves " to one " Pater Noster." Nay,
the case of Mary is singular in this entire humility and
humiliation. For we may all irrationally and nearly uncon-
sciously attribute some glory of genius to the poet, for
instance, as though it were his own by origin; but in the
case of the Mother of Christ there is no such vague illusion.
The little idolatries that are offered to the poet or the soldier
are withheld from her who is pre-eminent only for sanctity
bestowed, and distinguished only by her office assigned, the
preparation therefor, and the reward thereafter. And this
similitude of Mary and the moon is so perfect that it is a
wonder the simple should need, or the churches erect,
images of the Virgin of Nazareth, the Virgin of the
Annunciation, the Mother of the Seven Sorrows, or Our
Lady of Peace, or the Mother of Christ by His Cross,
or Mary under any invocation whatever, when, month by
month, newly lighted every month, the moon presents her
absolute similitude, her image with the superscription of
her Lord. And yet there is a nation with a noble language
that incredibly makes the moon masculine, facing—with
effrontery—a feminine sun.

   The natural love of all ages for a Mother is obviously
older than the Christian love of nineteen centuries for a
perpetual Virgin. Therefore Mary, her Virginity receiving
all its mystery and all its singular glory from the fact of her
Maternity, is closest to the heart of sorrowful mankind by
the title of Mother. On her Virginity the meditations of
Christian men have brooded, moreover, with untired delight,

because it is a character of joy; to it belongs the "Joyful
Mystery"; to her Maternity the chief of the "Sorrowful."
Maternity in the world is the saddest thing in it. Not the
"Mother of Sorrows" is the most sorrowful of mothers.
For Judas had a mother, and Borgia, and the rich man of the
parable—if he was no more than a type, then all the actual
rich men for whom he stood—and the man who beats his
wife and his children, had mothers. Furthermore, many
women of our melancholy century are out of the reach of the
kindness of the words of Christ : " A woman hath sorrow
because her hour has come; but when she is delivered of
the child she remembereth no more the anguish for joy that
a man is born into the world." These, for their little love,
these again, for their great love, of children and their distrust
of life, undergo a sorrow not foreseen by nature—rather a
sorrow than a joy that a man is born into the world.

V. TRADITION

IT is not to the present purpose to attempt a distinction
between more and less authorized legends. Englishmen have been long accustomed to the abrupt division
whereby the Church once for all set the canonical Gospels
apart, and have heartily accepted it. The Apocryphal Gospels
have had little interest in England for any but students; and
the differences between traditions that have almost Scrip-
tural authority and the wholly unauthorized legends of later
times are still more particularly a matter for expert scholarship. When English readers, or English people in galleries
abroad, leave what is for them the safe old ground of the
four Evangelists, all the rest is indifferent to them; they are
either a little curious or a little incurious—generally a little
incurious.

They may follow Raphael, for instance, as far as the
Espousals of Mary and Joseph, for in the Scriptures there is
mention of the Espousals, but they do not ask with much
interest, if they ask at all, what the other men, in the famous,
the once over-praised Sposalizio in the Brera, are about—
young men breaking sticks across their knees. It is more than
probable that many a " Nativity of the Virgin " is taken for
a variant of the Nativity of Christ, painted by some master
who had become weary of the presence of the ox and the ass,
had had enough of the loft or the cave, of the shepherds and
Saint Joseph, and was minded to provide the birth of the
Saviour with credible witnesses in the form of women busy
in sick-room offices about the Mother and Child. And yet
those women are, in Tradition, all provided with names—
friends and handmaids of St. Anne. For them noble Floren-
tines lent their beauty and their costumes, not indeed as

standing models, but as suggestions, walking by in gala, and
affording to the painter the pattern of fine bearing and the
visiting dress of "high life." Nothing remains, in the popular
mind of our country, except the long habit of the name of
Anne : Mary and Anne, names of the fairer daughter and
the fair mother, and Mary Anne, the name whereby a child
was placed under the double patronage. But few of the Annes
of modern England have referred their grave and homely
monosyllable to the wife of Joachim and the aged mother of
Mary. Joachim, by the way, seems to have taken no possession of the English boy.

The tradition is, then, that Anne, wedded to Joachim,
was a woman growing old, and living childless. Here is the
often repeated story of the husband and wife hoping in vain
for a child, until the day of hope was at an end.

The Apocryphal gospel of Saint James Minor relates that
Joachim, a rich man, offered gifts in the Temple in abun-
dance, and that on such a festival-day, as he appeared with
others, the priest Reuben refused his alms, saying " Thou
shalt bring nothing to the treasure, who hast no child in
Israel." Joachim was filled with grief, the more as he saw
that all the just men of his tribe had sons and daughters.
He departed to the desert and prayed there and fasted forty
days. Meanwhile Anne, his wife, was weeping for her
barrenness. As the same festival approached again Judith,
her handmaid, would have prepared her for going abroad,
and she, having refused, at last consented. She allowed her
mourning raiment to be taken away, tired her head, and
suffered her attendant to put upon her a wedding garment.
Towards the ninth hour Anne went down into her garden
and walked there, sat under a laurel, and prayed. Lifting
her eyes she perceived in the branches of the laurel a nest
of sparrows, and wept anew for her misfortune when she saw
how fruitful were those birds, and considered how the fruitful fishes filled the seas, and the fruitful beasts the land.
Then did an Angel of the Lord fly forth to tell her that she

too should have the felicity of motherhood; two other Angels, moreover, warned her to look for the home-coming of Joachim, who was then returning from the mountain with his flocks. Anne, no longer in tears, ran to meet him and joyously threw her arms about his neck. Soon afterwards the priest was moved to accept his gift; and in due time was born his daughter Mary.

This story of the unauthorized "Gospel," with many variants, was the popular legend of the Nativity of Mary. According to the Gnostic legend, Anne made her lamentation within doors, upon her knees, and Joachim, being abroad, was bidden by an Angel to make an offering to God of a white lamb, and the Angel went back into Heaven in the smoke of the sacrifice. Seeing this, Joachim fell on his face and so remained until the evening. Rising, he told his shepherds what had happened, who rejoiced with him, and after thirty days' journey with the lingering and feeding flocks, the patriarch drew near to the Golden Gate of the city of Jerusalem, and there he was welcomed by his wife Anne, who had gone out with her maids to await her husband's coming.

The Greek Menology, now in the Vatican Library, also tells and pictures the story thus. Here, in the Nativity picture, we see Anne laid in her bed in an open chamber, three women bringing food to her bedside, another making ready to wash the girl-baby, and testing, nurse-like, with her hand the temperature of the water. The composition has some of the last beauty of Antiquity. It suggests a derivation from an ancient bas-relief representing the horoscope of a child in the presence of the Fates. The ministering woman in charge of the child, says Professor Venturi, "represents the slave who appears in the antique bas-reliefs, one of the group in the natal chamber, about to wash the infant Achilles, or whatever hero has entered into the world. Again in a fragment of a sarcophagus . . . one slave is intent upon the washing of the baby, and the three Fates are present at the birth, the first with a globe, the second with tablets, the third with the distaff and spindle." It is enough to warn the student here that he cannot read the work of Giotto in Padua or of Giovanni da Milano in Florence, nor indeed the "literature," as the art-critics of yesterday would say, of any of the masters earlier and later, without making himself well acquainted with Joachim and Anne, and with the handmaids of their household; especially with Judith, the cheerful girl who lifted Anne from her despondency, and arrayed her for the return of Joachim, saying "Surely as I am thy handmaid, thou hast the form and beauty of a queen." Milan Cathedral is dedicated not precisely to the Nativity of Mary, but to Mary Nascent—*Mariæ Nascenti*.

The Middle Ages were everywhere devout, as Brittany is to-day, to "The Lady Saint Anne." The feast was liturgically kept in the eleventh and twelfth centuries, but it lapsed, or rather was suppressed, for we read that it was "restored" by Pope Gregory XIII in A.D. 1584. A manuscript of the year 1031, in the British Museum, gives evidence of the observance of the feast at that date. The reason of the temporary suppression, by Pius V, in A.D. 1568, was the necessity of precaution against the random legends derived from the Apocryphal Gospels; these were finding their wandering way into the liturgical offices. Order was put therein, and the commemoration of Saint Anne then reinstated. But the Eastern Church seems to have kept it without intermission, from the third century onwards.

The second legendary history is that of the Presentation of Mary in the Temple. It will be seen that these "mysteries" of the Mother are copied from the pattern of those of the Son. Of the Presentation of Mary everyone is bound to know something, in these days of little books of art, if only because of Titian and Tintoretto and the two great rival pictures. But there is much legend surrounding that incident. When Anne had weaned her daughter, says an Apocryphal Gospel in the chapters of the Nativity, she went with Joachim to

F

the Temple and there she left the child Mary that she might grow up among the maidens abiding there night and day praising the Lord. When the child was brought before the Temple, she walked up the stairs (fifteen stairs, we are told, there were) without turning round or crying for her mother. All that saw it were filled with wonder. Another version relates that Mary was three years old when she was presented in the Temple, and this reading, as the more manageable, Titian and Tintoretto, Giotto, Bartoli di Fredi, the Homilies of James the Monk, and indeed all painters have followed—almost; their little maiden is of walking age; she might be of ages between four and fourteen. Mary went up with other little virgins bearing her company, and surpassed them in favour as the sun surpasses the stars. Zacharias was the priest who received her.

In course of time the High Priest set about the weaving of the veil of the Temple. He entrusted the threads of gold, scarlet, and right purple to maidens of the House of David, and to the share of Mary fell the purple. She took it away to spin in her own home about the time of her espousals to Saint Joseph. With that betrothal the zeal and chivalry of Romance played most joyously and with manly devotion. Zacharias called together all the young men of Jerusalem desiring to marry, so that he might choose one worthy of the most pious and the most beautiful of the maids in his care. They flocked to the competition, and he bade each to bring a rod, expecting a sign of the choice of God. He took all the rods in his hand, entered the Temple, and prayed there, and returning gave to each man his own again, until he came to Joseph, when he found that his rod had flowered. A variant relates that a dove was seen to rest upon the head of the Saint. Zacharias said to him: " Thou art chosen by God to take His Virgin: take her home and guard her." Some little confusion occurs here in the legends, inasmuch as we are told that Saint Joseph had presented himself as a suitor, and also that he answered the High Priest, " I have sons and am an old man; whereas she is young. I would not bring on myself the derision of the young men of Israel." But the High Priest reminded him of the chastisements inflicted by God upon those who refused to do His will. Joseph therefore received the young Virgin, saying, " I will take thee to my house, then I will go to my labour, and later return to thee."

According to the unauthorized Gospel of the Nativity, which differs from the Apocryphal Gospel of St. James already cited, the suitors numbered about three thousand. The High Priest was named Abiathar; receiving no sign on his prayer over the rods of the young men, he put on the sacred vestment with twelve bells and went into the Holy Place to offer sacrifice. There an angel appeared to him and said, " Behold this smallest rod of all, which thou hast left aside. When thou shalt restore it to him who brought it there shall be given to thee a sign." The little rod was Joseph's, and he stood in his humility the last of the great multitude of suitors. Then Abiathar called him in a loud voice. Joseph came, full of fear, and when he put forth his hand to take the rod, there came from it a white dove that flew awhile round the eaves of the Temple and then took its course into the cloud. All the people rejoiced with him and said to him, " Thou art happy in thy old age, since God hath called thee to be betrothed to Mary." The priests said to him, " Take her, for God hath chosen thee." With great misgiving Joseph answered, " I am old, and I have many sons. Why do you give me so young a bride?" And, the chronicler again forgetting to account for his entering upon the competition, Joseph is shown to us still protesting; he would ask for a sign for one of his sons, since it seemed that Mary should come into his house. This being denied, he asked that certain virgins should accompany her, to afford her young society; and five were chosen: Rebecca, Saphora, Susanna, Abigea, and Zaele. (Five, too, are the virgins in Rossetti's lovely poem, whose names are " five sweet symphonies." We may therefore suppose this poet to have been acquainted with the legend.) These handmaids were to dwell with Joseph and Mary, and to spin.

The writers of the Apocryphal Gospels and the Greek Fathers alike assign to Saint Joseph no more than the charge of guarding the youth of Mary. The Latins, on the other hand, admit a formal espousal, which is certainly according to the canonical Gospel of Saint Luke. " A virgin espoused to Joseph " is a phrase that seems to denote a devoted maidenhood followed by a marriage. The delicate Dark Ages and Middle Ages, it may be noted, in the excessive sweetness and refinement of thought that makes the modern world, the "civilized," seem by comparison ruffianly indeed, interpret the whole history most sensitively. In the teeth of the Apocryphal Gospels themselves, Joseph had been a celibate saint to his old age; and Mary Magdalen was no gross outcast and sinner of the streets—she was only a rather vain young woman who loved too much to look out of the window and to dress. But so good were the people of the Holy Land, said the mediæval Italian preacher, that such light conduct was terrible in their eyes. And the homage of the age to the Innocence—nay, to the mere beauty—of Mary it was that thronged her door with suitors—with a thousand, nay, with three thousand. It was hard for the devout imagination of chivalry to stop at three thousand. Scruples or simplicities are these that make mirth for the modern clown.

VI. TRADITION (II)

SO far Tradition brings us to the door of the room, or to the gate of the garden, to the threshold of the palace gallery or of the cell, in which the Angelic salutation and the Virginal reply were spoken.

Here then we are on Biblical ground, but Tradition and popular legend slip into the history. The Apocryphal Gospel of St. James Minor, already cited, relates that Mary was in the act of drawing water from a well when she heard the " Hail " of the announcing voice. The Virgin looked to right and left and saw not who spoke to her. Afraid, she went into the house, set down her water-vessel, and sat to spin her purple. Then, in the sheltered house the Angel took shape, and Saint Luke tells the rest. The Apocryphal Gospel of the Nativity adds this thought—that Mary was well accustomed to the faces of Angels, and to the apparition of the splendour of these heavenly visitants. It is, as far as I know, a rarely written, but it is not an unpainted, apocryphal tradition that gives to the Annunciation a witness, in the person of one of the five handmaidens of Mary, who draws a curtain within the holy house, and overhears the salutation and the colloquy.

When Mary is represented, in painting, on her knees at the entrance of Gabriel, this is in accordance with the Apocryphal Gospel that tells us of her practice of prayer. She prayed from daybreak until the third hour, laboured from the third hour to the ninth, and after the ninth hour resumed her prayer, her studies of the Law, and singing of the Psalms of David. Tertullian had said that the Word went forth from God as a ray of light, the Christian hymnologists had named Mary the gate of light, and had sung of her conception of the Son by a shadow or a breath from God. And Peire de Corbiac, taking his inspiration from the Latin hymns, in his song upon the " Lady Queen of Angels," tells how " *intra bels rais quan solelha per la fenestra veirina* " ("the fair rays entered in as the sun shines in at a window of glass ").

The Visitation of the Virgin to her cousin Saint Elizabeth follows immediately upon the Annunciation in the Gospel narrative. We read that after the message of the Angel, Mary arose and went in haste towards the mountain city of Juda. " And she entered into the house of Zachary, and saluted Elizabeth. And it came to pass that when Elizabeth heard the salutation of Mary, the infant leaped in her womb. And Elizabeth was filled with the Holy Ghost: and she cried out with a loud voice, and said, Blessed art thou among women, and blessed is the fruit of thy womb. And whence is this to me, that the mother of my Lord should come to me? And blessed art thou who hast believed, because those things shall be accomplished that were spoken to thee by the Lord."

Mary replied with the celestial hymn that we call by its first word in the Latin version, " *Magnificat.*" After abiding with Elizabeth three months, she returned to her own home. The celebration of the festival of the Visitation dates from the seventh century, but its representation in art is found in sixth-century work in the chair of Maximian at Ravenna. Tradition surrounds the figures of the two women with attendants; Elizabeth stands with Zacharias, Mary comes with Joseph, handmaids, servants, and a laden ass. With the succeeding " Anxieties of Saint Joseph " tradition has dealt also. To the history of the Gospel Saint James Minor adds that Joseph wept and was in tribulation, and that after his reassurance he was accused by a scribe before the High Priest, who caused him to drink, in company with Mary, the bitter water commanded by the law of Moses. The Gospel of the Nativity says moreover that Joseph and Mary, having taken the water of ordeal, and walked seven times about the altar of the Lord, were so manifestly innocent that all the people acclaimed them.

Soon follows the Nativity. Literal at once and mystical, the Middle Ages are all-precise. The general ox, the general ass, that, in the monitory Scripture, know their Master's crib while Israel " doth not consider," became for them the one ox, the one ass, that in fact stood at the crib of the Master when Israel did not consider Him. By another interpretation this ox and this ass are symbols of the Jew and the Gentile—the Jew still bound under the burden of the law, and the heathen loaded with the oppression of idolatry. And in yet another Apocryphal Gospel—that of a pseudo Saint Matthew, compiled from Greek sources (as was also the narrative of " Thomas the Israelite ") towards the sixth century, we read that the Divine Child was in fact adored in the manger by the ox and the ass. In vain was the pseudo-gospel condemned by Pope Gelasius; the legendary incidents of the Nativity had taken fast hold of the popular mind. The writer—the pretended Saint Matthew—adds to the interest of his story by names: Zelomi and Salome were handmaids of Mary who were present at the Nativity. Salome had her arm withered because she had doubted of the honour of the Mother of the Lord, but on her repentance it was restored. On that holy night "The lambs stood still in the way," runs an Apocryphal story; " the shepherd lifted up his staff to drive them forward, but his hand was staid; and at the waters of the brook the goats would not drink, but stood, and their mouths were open." More is told of the Wise Men than of the Shepherds. Their names—Caspar, Melchior, and Balthasar—have passed into frequent baptismal use in Italy. One was old, one was young, and one a negro. Saint Ephrem, in his Canticle, relates that Mary was troubled at the coming of these Wise Kings, fearing lest they should prove to be emissaries of tyranny, and lest Herod might intend to pluck this tender fruit of the vine before its hour of maturity. She asked them wherefore they had left their own countries to bring their treasure to her Child; and they answered her that they had travelled thither in order to pay their homage to the King of kings. "And how is this," she rejoined, "that a poor woman has given birth to a King? I have naught, my house is empty and poor. My Babe has no throne, no jewels, no legions; He lies in the poverty of His mother."

To the Gospel history of the Purification of the Virgin and the Presentation of Our Lord, the Apocryphal writers made their own additions. The story of the Childhood shows us the aged Simeon visited by the apparition of a pillar of light, in the midst whereof was the Child, while Mary, at the moment of receiving back her Son from the priest, appeared surrounded by a circle of rejoicing angels. The writer of "The Nativity of Mary" describes Simeon in adoration of the Child; he takes Jesus in his mantle and kisses the soles of His feet, crying: "God has visited His people."

Yet another Apocryphal history is that of "Joseph the Carpenter." The writer puts the narrative into the mouth of Christ Himself: "Joseph arose and took my mother Mary, and carried me in his arms. And Salome followed them upon their way into Egypt; and there, forsaking his own country, he abode a year." The same is told, much less simply, in the gospel of "The Holy Infancy," which became well known through the French translation made in the thirteenth century. According to this legend, the idols of the Egyptians fell to the ground at the passing of the Son of God, the air was full of the music of instruments as at the coming of a King, a new spring of water welled up at the foot of a sycamore tree, monsters vanished, robbers took flight, and the earth brought forth balsam for the healing of the sick. The Child was worshipped by lions, leopards, wolves, and dragons. On the third day of the journey Mary was weary in the desert because of the heat of the sun; and seeing a tree she said to Joseph: "Let us rest awhile in the shadow." Joseph made haste to lift her from the saddle. Being seated, Mary raised her eyes to the branches of the palm, and seeing them covered with fruit she said: "If it were possible I would gladly eat some of these dates." And

"I AM THE MOTHER OF FAIR LOVE AND OF HOLY HOPE"

he said, "I marvel at thy saying, seeing how high grow those dates, and how far out of reach." Then the Child Jesus, being in His Mother's arms, said to the palm-tree, "Bow thy branches, and nourish her with thy fruits." Immediately the palm-tree bent down its topmost branches even to the feet of Mary.

As the hour of the Passion and Death of Our Saviour drew near tradition was again at work where the Scriptures are silent, and one of the scenes reconstructed in meditation and commentary was that of the leave-taking of Christ when He left His Mother before the beginning of His Sacrifice. The profoundest and most beautiful of all Correggio's works, the picture in which the usually self-satisfied and too graceful Correggio is himself greatly moved—shows this leave-taking. The Saviour kneels for a blessing at His Mother's feet. She, with a deathly face, gives it, and Mary Magdalen holds her up. At the foot of the Cross she rejoined Him.

In the poem, of remoter antiquity, erroneously attributed to Saint Gregory Nazianzen, the Virgin receives the grateful praises of her Son, with His exhortation to shed no tears, for all that had been foretold in the prophecies must come to pass. And Mary, full of admiration of the generosity and sanctity of Christ, who pardons on the Cross, replies that through three nights she will look for the rising of the sun and for the fulfilment of the promise. But when the Son makes no answer she cries, "Would to God that for Thy soul I had given mine, which I care not for. Now does darkness cover mine eyes; without Thee I desire to be buried, and to be hidden in the earth. In vain, then, did I nurse Thee, my Son. . . . No longer may I stand and look upon Thee. Wherefore art thou silent? Speak yet again to Thy Mother!" On her maternal grief when Christ is dead devout imagination has dealt with many conjectures. The *Acta Pilati* tell of her fainting, the Venerable Bede of her falling with her face to the ground. In the thoughts of others she stands erect throughout the three hours. In the hour of the

Deposition tradition assigns to her the releasing of the right hand of the Crucified, while Nicodemus drew the nails from the left hand and from the feet. The *Pietà* is entirely traditional; so is the presence of Mary at the Sepulchre. With the mention of her prayer in the gathering of the Apostles in the expectation of Pentecost, the New Testament leaves her, her name, and her office to silence, until the day of the Revelation of Saint John. In that mystical day the theology of centuries sees her in the great wonder in Heaven: "A woman clothed with the sun and having the moon under her feet."

But Tradition follows her from the Sepulchre to the Mount of the Ascension; into the house of John; and into the ceremonial chamber of her ritual death—her "sleep," as the Christian ages called it—when the Angel who had brought her the lily of her consecrated maidenhood brought her the palm of her long martyrdom of maternal love. Dante, however, speaks of the palm, not the lily, of the Annunciation, but all the painters after his date choose the lily. One tradition assigns the annunciation of death to Michael, not to Gabriel.

The Apocryphal Gospel is not content with the gathering together at Mary's death-bed of such friends and followers of Christ as were in Jerusalem, but miraculously brings thither all the scattered Apostles from the nations of the Gentiles. As John was preaching in Ephesus, suddenly it thundered out of Heaven, and a white cloud covered the Evangelist, and carried him to the death-chamber of Mary. He knocked upon the door, entered in, and greeted his Mother who wept with joy to see him, and reminded him of the word spoken upon the Cross which entrusted the Mother to the friend. And she committed to the Beloved Disciple the care of her pure body after death, so that the Jews should not—as they had plotted—carry away and cast into the flames the body that had conceived and carried Christ. At the same hour the thunder sounded, and all the

MARY IN THE SANCTUARY

Apostles, brought in like manner in clouds from the places where they were then preaching, entered into the chamber of Mary to be present at death's Annunciation. John told them that the Virgin was near to her joy and her reward, and stanching his own tears enjoined upon them that they should not weep. Peter stood at her head, and John at her feet, and the other Apostles round about. When it was the third hour of the night, thunder struck the house until it shook, and the chamber was filled with a fragrance so sweet that many were faint and overcome with sleep. In that awful hour Christ Himself entered. With Him were Angels, Patriarchs, Prophets, Virgins, and the Martyrs who had already suffered for His Name's sake. All drew near to the bed of Mary, and Christ said to His dear Mother, " Come, thou chosen amongst all women." And Mary answered, "Lord, my heart is ready." All those present sang a canticle, and Mary herself sang a verse of her own " Magnificat": "All generations shall call me blessed, for He that is mighty hath done to me great things." And Christ spoke, " My beloved, come from Lebanon and receive thy crown." Mary said, " Thou art all my joy."

Upon this, her spiritual Assumption, followed the tradition of her bodily Assumption, with which in the course of ages all Christendom seems to ring.

But the meditation that followed the Mother of Christ through the gates of death went beyond, and saw her crowned as the Queen and Mother of Saints. All who had done the Will of God and were therefore, according to Christ's own word, His mothers and sisters and brothers, gave honour to her whom her Son crowned in eternity, as His mother by a double title, having borne Him and having done the Will of God, the greatest Will of God, perfectly. Beyond the Coronation and the close of the history of Mary, moreover—beyond the past and the present, the thoughts of all the Christian countries followed the Mother prophetically to her prayers in the future, at the very Judgement Seat of

Christ. It is perhaps rather to the painted than to the written testimony that we owe the record of this prophecy.

Albeit Pope Gelasius had put forth his hand to check the impetuous faith of the generations which were in so much generous haste to fulfil to the utmost the prophecy of Mary, and to call her blessed in Assumption and Coronation, as well as in Child-bearing and in the transfixing of her soul at the foot of the Cross, the popular acclamation carried the fame of those newer mysteries. The devout of the Middle Ages might have used Newman's reasoning on religious evolution, or Galileo's traditional but now disproved reply to another Pontiff, " *Eppur si muove*."

It should be added that no attempt has been made in these pages to reproduce the labours of scholarship in regard to the age or authority of traditions, or the authorship of the apocryphal New Testament writings. The popular and lasting legends accepted in Europe have been here simply recorded as they stand.

VII. POETRY

THE whole world would not contain the books that might be written of the mere three years of Our Saviour's work on earth, says His Beloved Disciple, speaking with the sudden hyperbole that surprises us at the end of his Gospel of contained and mastered emotion. It is because he is the one Evangelist who does comment, and explain, who turns the leaf back and adds an afterthought; who undertook to answer for the two most mystical of the miracles—the Transubstantiation at Cana and the Raising of Lazarus—who, moreover, took upon himself the record of the words of Christ in the upper chamber and of the singing of the hymn, and in whose recital we are aware of the breaking heart of the friend of Christ; it is because we know him so spiritual, and so exalted, that the extravagant and enthusiastic phrase startles and delights us.

Why then did he who knew so much that his knowledge caused him to write thus fantastically, set down so little? But for that scantiness his posterity and the posterity of all Evangelists and all Apostles have sought to make amends. The world of books has hardly been able to contain what has been written about the Gospels; the before and after of the Gospels; the systems, the speculation, the teaching, the followings, the revolts. The prophecy of Simeon must be fulfilled, and the thoughts of many hearts have been revealed. The thoughts of many hearts have been set down; literatures have lived in honour of Christ; literatures have been composed in honour of Mary, and the hymns of the liturgy, the immortal offices of her festivals. The liturgies stand, once for all; but besides these are the libraries filled with commentary and meditation, entrusted like the liturgies, to the Greek of the Oriental churches, and to the Latin of the Occidental. And after these, the vulgar tongues.

The adequate translation of poetry in verse—and especially the translation of the poetry of a polysyllabic language into the verse of one largely monosyllabic, as, for example, of Italian poetry into English, is virtually impossible. The brevity of the polysyllabic line must needs be rendered by the diffuseness and languor in the monosyllabic—a fact obvious enough, and not a paradox. No attempt therefore will be made here to present any but English verse. The world is full of theology that has made a commentary, and of poetry that has made a chorus, for the resounding song of the " Magnificat." Of all this, the theology is beyond the reach of the present essay, and the poetry is strangely divided. Every love-song of the Middle Ages that is a love-song indeed was written in final honour of Mary. In Guido Cavalcanti's lovely lines the ladies who followed his lady seemed to him not so truly ladies as shadows, because they walked near her; but his lady in her turn was a shadow of the Lady of all Christian men. Humility and Sanctity are the virtues and honours of the beloved woman because Mary was the pattern of sanctity and humility. Italy's divine poets who were of one mind with Dante—who needed no personal alliance with him in order to think with him, so indisputable was it that sanctity and humility were worshipful and to be ascribed to the lady who had possession of a man's heart—Italy's heavenly-minded poets, I say, were early poets; and England, coming later into the company of poets, lost the Mary of the older Christendom. Mary had little part in the "spacious days"; the votaries of Elizabeth were not hers; and our incomparable literature was dispossessed of that human ideal. Shakespeare indeed restored or retained it; his unparalleled mind effected an imaginative immaculate conception of absolute sanctity and innocence intact : Cordelia—Virgo potens ; Isabel—Virgo

prudentissima; Miranda, Perdita—Virgo veneranda, Virgo
prædicanda, Virgo fidelis ; Hermione—Mater admirabilis,
Mater intemerata ; Desdemona, Imogen—Vas honorabile,
Fœderis arca, Speculum justitiæ. These women divide
amongst themselves the titles of a litany all the invocations
of which together were appropriate to one alone. Shakespeare divides the titles, the virtues, the benedictions ;
separates them, makes them humanly credible by sharing
them, ascribes them, and cherishes them. They are scattered
by his generous hand, but they are not changed.

Even thus divided, however, they did not long shine or
survive in poetry. Milton's Eve has a different honour, a
different duty, an altogether different beauty. The lady of
the Middle Ages, the lady who was the shadow of Mary,
Mary herself who spoke the Magnificat, never spoke thus
to man :

> My author and disposer, what thou bidst
> Unargued I obey; so God ordains;
> God is thy law, thou mine.

Of all the changes of the mind of mankind in regard to the
duty and the mind of women—I say of mankind rather
than of man, because women and men have shared the
change, and have thought alike on this matter—none can
be greater than the change from the mediæval thought to
the puritan, from Guido Cavalcanti's rapturous poem to the
Vicar of Wakefield and its women, and from the Gospel
according to Saint Luke to Genesis according to Milton.

The education of women sank quickly from the date of
the beginning of Puritanism, until it became what it was in
Deborah, the intolerable and, worse, the tolerated, wife of
Goldsmith's Vicar. Artificial inequality became the custom
of England when Mary was dismissed.

Thus there is less in our rich Letters than in those of
poorer countries, in honour of sanctity, humility, honour,
and responsibility in women. The good women of our older
novelists are not responsible nor honourable, and the fairly

good women of our later fiction are not humble nor holy.
There was one institution that recognized with all authority
and power, and with every heavy sanction, the responsibility
of every woman, and it is the institution that, inevitably
and of course, the man made by puritanism—the man of
Milton—proscribed, denounced, and abolished. I mean, of
course, the Confessional. Let us imagine, if we can, Eve
going to Confession—taking her separate soul, say to the
Archangel Michael—and what Milton's Adam would say
to it.

The loss to literature has been something other than the
cessation of hymns. These have, in fact, not ceased.
Coventry Patmore said that no good hymns had been
written since the Council of Trent—a sweeping judgement
to which there are surely exceptions. But a wider loss than
that of hymns has been the loss of the distribution among
good women by generous men of the titles and invocations
aforesaid. That is a loss for which no increase or enlarge-
ment of liberty can make amends. It is a loss not only of
yesterday, not only of last century or of the eighteenth
century. The "early Victorian" woman, over whose timidity
and fainting, and so forth, cries of triumph and improve-
ment are now tediously repeated, suffered that loss no less
than her more intelligent, more courageous, and more
arrogant successor. The loss is now some four centuries
old. A sub-derisive tone is all too audible in the life of
our world. The most admired woman, or the woman admired by the greater number, is now doubtless the actress.
But the praises of her beauty are in *argot*. Loveliness
that can hardly be less than that of Helen of Troy walks
the silly stage, serves in the dull shop, or dresses and dances
appraised but unadored. It is assuredly because Virgo
Potens, Virgo Clemens, Vas Insigne Devotionis, Mater
Divinæ Gratiæ, Janua Cæli are titles that have ceased to
be gathered in honour of one that they have ceased to be
scattered in honour of many.

Within our age nevertheless—in the latest years of the nineteenth century—two poets have gathered and distributed those titles of honour. None in any time, Guido Cavalcanti and Dante excepted, has gathered more devoutly and distributed more nobly. Coventry Patmore, because he sang of "ladies' graces"—the participations, obscure, uncertain—because he sang flattering songs and hyperbolical, attributing more beauty than is quite possible, here to a girl, there to a wife—Virgo Veneranda, Salus Infirmorum—was able, when the day came and the occasion, to collect his praises and bind them together for the Mother of Christ. "Ah, Lady elect," he cries, with the one and unexpected pang of irony at the outset of a tender poem, "whom the Time's scorn has saved from its respect,"

> Grant me the steady heat
> Of thought, wise, splendid, sweet,
> Urged by the great, rejoicing wind that rings
> With draught of unseen wings,
> Making each phrase, for love and for delight,
> Twinkle like Sirius on a frosty night!
> Aid then thy own dear fame, thou only Fair,
>   At whose petition meek
> The Heavens themselves decree that, as it were,
>   They will be weak!
>
> Thou speaker of all wisdom in a Word—
>   Thy Lord!
> Speaker who thus couldst well afford
> Thence to be silent! Ah, what silence that,
> Which had for prologue thy "Magnificat"!
>   O silence full of wonders
> More than by Moses on the Mount were heard,
> More than were utter'd by the seven thunders;
> Silence that crowns, unnoted, like the voiceless blue,
>   The loud world's varying view,
> And in its holy heart the sense of all things ponders!
>   That acceptably I may speak of thee,
>   Ora pro me!
>
> *   *   *   *   *
>
> My lady, yea, the Lady of my Lord,
>   Who didst the first descry

The burning secret of virginity,
　　We know with what reward,

*　　　*　　　*　　　*　　　*

To One, thy Husband, Father, Son, and Brother,
Spouse blissful, Daughter, Sister, milk-sweet Mother,
　　　　Ora pro me !

*　　　*　　　*　　　*　　　*

Creature of God rather the sole than first;
　　Knot of the cord
Which binds together all and all unto their Lord;
　　Suppliant omnipotence,
Peace-beaming star, by which shall come enticed
　　Unto thy Babe's small feet
The Mighty, wandering disemparadised !

Here again is part of a modern poem, Rossetti's "Ave,"
written by one who would not have written it unless he had
attributed exquisite virtue to a living woman, "Love-Lily,"
and tears to the lady looking from Heaven. Love-Lily is
the mortal maid

Whose thought Truth knows not from her word,
Nor Love her body from her soul.

And the Blessed Damozel weeps "tears of patience, dumb
and slow." Because Rossetti was one of the three who in
our time have divided the honours of Mary, in mystical
quality and in heroic degree, among mortal women, he was
able, when to him too came the day and the occasion, to
give for ever to all lovers of virtue his heavenly poem:

Mind'st thou not (when the twilight gone
Made darkness in the house of John),
Between the naked window-bars
That spacious vigil of the stars?—
For thou, a watcher even as they,
Wouldst rise from where throughout the day
Thou wroughtest raiment for His poor;
And, finding the fixed terms endure
Of day and night which never brought
Sounds of His coming chariot,
Wouldst lift through cloud-wastes unexplored
Those eyes which said "How long, O Lord?"

REST ON THE FLIGHT INTO EGYPT

Then that disciple whom He loved,
Well heeding, haply might be moved
To ask thy blessing in His name;
And that one thought in both, the same,
Though silent, then would clasp ye round
To weep together,—tears long bound,
Sick tears of patience, dumb and slow.
Yet, "Surely I come quickly,"—so
He said, from life and death gone home.
Amen: even so, Lord Jesus, come!
But Oh! what human tongue can speak
That day when Michael came to break
From the tir'd spirit, like a veil,
Its covenant with Gabriel
Endured at length unto the end?
What human thought can apprehend
That mystery of motherhood
When thy Beloved at length renewed
The sweet communion severed,—
His left hand underneath thine head,
And His right hand embracing thee?—
Lo! He was thine, and this is He!
Soul, is it Faith or Love or Hope
That lets me see her standing up
Where the light of the throne is bright?

    *   *   *   *   *

O Mary Mother, be not loth
To listen,—thou whom the stars clothe,
Who seest and mayst not be seen!
Hear us at last, O Mary Queen!
Into our shadow bend thy face,
Bowing thee from the secret place,
O Mary Virgin, full of grace!

"First Love Remembered," the romance of Rose Mary, "Love-Lily," the passionate pilgrimage of "Staff and Scrip," were the poems that helped the poet to this spiritual song. In like manner, Coventry Patmore rehearsed, in honour of living women, his Ode for the Virgin, and in like manner Francis Thompson rehearsed, in "Love in Dian's Lap," written for one woman, the "Passion of Mary" and "Assumpta Maria." In the poem last named Mary speaks:

Multitudinous ascend I,
   Dreadful as a battle arrayed,

I

For I bear you whither tend I;
  Ye are I; be undismayed!
I, the ark that for the graven
  Tables of the Law was made;
Man's own heart was one, one Heaven,—
  Both within my womb were laid.

I, the flesh-girt paradises
  Gardenered by the Adam new,
Daintied o'er with sweet devices
  Which He loveth, for He grew.
I, the boundless strict savannah
  Which God's leaping feet go through;
I, the heaven whence the manna,
  Weary Israel, slid on you.

I am Daniel's mystic mountain,
  Whence the mighty stone was rolled;
I am the four rivers' fountain,
  Watering Paradise of old;
Cloud down-raining the Just One am,
  Danae of the Shower of Gold;
I the hostel of the sun am;
  He the Lamb, and I the fold.

Here the poet speaks in person:

See in highest heaven pavilioned
  Now the maiden Heaven rest,
The many-breasted sky out-millioned
  By the splendours of her vest.
Lo, the ark this holy tide is
  The un-handmade Temple's guest,
And the dark Egyptian bride is
  Whitely to the Spouse-heart prest.

*　　*　　*　　*　　*

Where is laid the Lord arisen?
  In the light we walk in gloom;
Though the sun has burst his prison,
  We know not his biding-room.
Tell us where the Lord sojourneth,
  For we find an empty tomb.
"Whence He sprang, there He returneth,
  Mystic Sun,—the Virgin's womb."

*　　*　　*　　*　　*

Who is she, in candid vesture,
   Rushing up from out the brine?
Treading, with resilient gesture,
   Air, and with that Cup divine?
She in us, and we in her are
   Beating Godward; all that pine;—
Lo! a wonder and a terror!
   The sun hath blushed the sea to wine!

Camp of angels! Well we even
   Of this thing may doubtful be,—
If thou art assumed to Heaven,
   Or is Heaven assumed to thee!
Consummatum. Christ, the promised,
   Thy maiden realm, is won, O strong!
Since to such sweet Kingdom comest,
   Remember me, poor Thief of song!

Conversely, it may be conjectured that the three poets
would not have written "Love-Lily," "Love in Dian's Lap,"
or "The Betrothal" if they had not made ready for "The
Child's Purchase," "Assumpta Maria," and "Ave." Where
would Crashaw's "Wishes for the Supposed Mistress" have
been but for his hymn "O Gloriosa Domina," or this last
have been but for the first? (A note to the whole suggestion
of the interplay of those two poetic actions—the gathering
for one woman, and the scattering for many women, of the
virtues and honours—may be added: It does not appear that
any woman poet has written memorable or exalted poetry in
the praise of Mary. Nor, accordingly, have women generally
exercised themselves in singing the praises even of the virtues
they love best, by way of tender flattery of their mortal fellow
women.)

But against all that has been here hazarded, the objection,
if not the refutation, is Shakespeare. He never gathered
Virgilia, Miranda, Viola, Cordelia, Portia, Perdita, Desdemona, Isabel, Juliet, Imogen, "a bundle of life," to be re-
commended to Mary, to be outdone and to be blessed by
her. Shakespeare thus puzzles our thoughts. He is here, as
he is often, the great exception.

Assuredly the literature that is of this world, of the passing age and the flying fashion, the literature that is shamed and condemned by the past and to be shamed and condemned by the future, has scattered among women other things than virtues. One virtue, even the smallest—"see, is it not a little one?"—which is modesty, is not attributed in popular fiction or in the popular poem to woman, thus despoiled at last of a little jewel worn for decorum rather than for splendour.

It is only from the poets of our time who have not followed the failing fashion that I have chosen the foregoing poetry to relieve so much dull prose. And let me add the brief "Assumption" of John Banister Tabb:

Behold! the Mother bird
The Fledgeling's voice hath heard!
    He calls anew,
    "It was thy breast
    That warmed the nest
    From whence I flew.
Upon a loftier tree
Of life I wait for thee;
Rise, Mother-dove, and come,
Thy Fledgeling calls thee home!"

And Robert Stephen Hawker's "Aishah Schechinah":

A shape, like folded light, embodied air,
    Yet wreathed with flesh, and warm;
All that of Heaven is feminine and fair
    Moulded in visible form.

She stood, the Lady Schechinah of Earth,
    A chancel for the sky;—
Where woke to breath and beauty, God's own birth,
    For men to see Him by.

Round her, too pure to mingle with the day,
    Light, that was Life, abode;
Folded within her fibres meekly lay
    The link of boundless God.

So linked, so blent, that when, with pulse fulfilled,
    Moved but that infant Hand,
Far, far away, His conscious Godhead thrilled,
    And stars might understand.

> Lo! where they pause, with intergathering rest,
>   The Threefold and the One!
> And lo! He binds them to her Orient breast,
>   His Manhood girded on.
>
> The Zone, where two glad worlds for ever meet,
>   Beneath that bosom ran:—
> Deep in that womb, the conquering Paraclete
>   Smote Godhead on to man!
>
> Sole scene among the stars, where, yearning, glide
>   The Threefold and the One:
> Her God upon her lap, the Virgin-Bride,
>   Her awful Child, her Son.

The tale of contemporary or very recent Marian poetry is thus soon ended. Allusions, however, in Katharine Tynan's lovely lyrics, are worth many poems; and one must not escape me. It is from the prayer of the mother, who knows herself to prop the house, to spread the table and the bed, to light the lamp and kindle the fire, and to cause all to live and thrive, above all the precious children:

> I am their wall against all danger,
>   Their door against the wind and snow.
> Thou, whom a woman laid in manger,
>   Take me not till the children grow.

And Mr. Chesterton, who wrote, "Chastity does not mean abstention from actual wrong; it means something flaming, like Joan of Arc," is aware of that "integrity of fire" which burnt at the heart of the Marian Middle Ages. Lionel Johnson prayed, in the lonely and holy, the awful but not unmanning, fear of death which was his:

> So, when the shadows come,
> Laden with all contrivances of fear,
>   Ah, Mary, lead us home
>   Through fear, through fire,
> To where with faithful companies we may hear
> That perfect music, which the love of God,
>   Who this dark way once trod,
> Creates among the imperishable choir.

Laurence Housman has brought a seventeenth-century
play time into our working world in his three stanzas on the
Annunciation, and Rudyard Kipling prays with his soldier,
his comrade, and his enemy:

> Ah, Mary, pierced with sorrow,
>   Remember, reach, and save
> The soul that comes to-morrow
>   Before the God that gave!

It is a long step backwards to Wordsworth's sonnet:

> Mother! whose virgin bosom was uncrosst
>   With the least shade of thought to sin allied;
>   Woman! above all women glorified,
> Our tainted nature's Solitary Boast;
> Purer than foam on central ocean tosst;
>   Brighter than eastern skies at daybreak strewn
>   With fancied roses, than the unblemished moon
> Before her wane begins on heaven's blue coast!
> Thy image falls to earth. Yet some, I ween,
>   Not unforgiven the suppliant knee might bend,
>   As to a visible power, in which did blend
> All that was mixed and reconciled in thee
> Of mother's love with maiden purity,
> Of high with low, celestial with serene.

And beyond Wordsworth it is a longer step to our ingen-
iously heavenly Crashaw. " *Sancta Maria Dolorum*," he calls
his poem, " or, the Mother of Sorrows; a pathetical Descant
upon the devout plainsong of *Stabat Mater Dolorosa*":

> In shade of Death's sad Tree
>   Stood doleful she;
> Ah, she! now by none other
> Name to be known, alas! but Sorrow's Mother.
>   Before her eyes
>   Hers and the whole world's Joys,
> Hanging, all torn, she sees, and in His woes
>   And pains, her pangs and throes;
> Each wound of His from every part
> All more at home in her own heart.
> What kind of marble then
>   Is that cold man
> Who can look on and see,

Nor keep such noble sorrows company?
    Sure, even from you,
    My flints, some drops are due,
To see so many unkind swords contest
    So far for one soft breast;
While with a faithful, mutual flood
Her eyes bleed tears, His wounds weep blood!

        *   *   *   *   *

    She sees her Son, her God,
    Bow with a load
Of borrowed sins, and swim
In woes that were not made for Him.
    Ah, hard command
    Of love! Here must she stand
Charged to look on, and with a steadfast eye
    See her Life die,
Leaving her only so much breath
As serves to keep alive her death.

    O Mother Turtle-dove!
    Soft source of love!
That these dry lids might borrow
Something from thy full seas of sorrow!
    O, in that breast
    Of thine (the noblest nest
Both of Love's fires and floods) might I recline
    This hard cold heart of mine!
The chill lump would relent, and prove
Soft subject for the siege of Love.

        *   *   *   *   *

    Yea, let my life and me
    Fix here with thee
And at the humble foot
Of this fair Tree take our eternal root,
    That so we may
    At least be in Love's way;
And in these chaste wars, while the winged wounds flee
    So fast 'twixt Him and thee,
My breast may catch the kiss of some kind dart,
Though at the second hand, from either heart.

        *   *   *   *   *

    Rich Queen, lend some relief,
    At least an alms to grief,
To a heart who, by sad right of sin,
Could prove the whole sum, too sure, due to Him.

By all those strings
  Of love, sweet bitter things,
Which these torn Hands transcribed on thy true heart,
  O, teach mine too the art
To study Him so, till we mix
Wounds, and become one crucifix.

  O, let me suck the wine
  So long of this chaste Vine,
Till, drunk of the dear wounds, I be
A lost thing to the world, as it to me!
  O faithful friend
  Of me, and of my end!
Fold up my life in love, and lay't beneath
  My dear Lord's vital Death.
Lo, heart, thy hope's whole plea—her precious breath
Poured out in prayer for thee; thy Lord's in death.

From Crashaw back to Ben Jonson is a shorter way—to
Herrick, to Southwell, to Donne, and to the lowlier names
of Englishmen of the times following the Reformation.
But the gaps are deep. We must go further, to the English
fifteenth century, for that most beautiful anonymous lyric:

I sing of a maiden
  That is makeless;
King of all Kings
  To her son she ches.

He came al so stille
  There his mother was,
As dew in Aprile
  That falleth on the grass.

He came al so stille
  To his mother's bour,
As dew in Aprile
  That falleth on the flour.

He came al so stille
  There his mother lay,
As dew in Aprile
  That falleth on the spray.

Mother and maiden
  Was never none but she;
Well may such a lady
  Goddes mother be.

There is, in Middle English, besides, many a lyrical prayer and cradle-song for Bethlehem scattered through a few centuries. Meanwhile the devotional and liturgical hymns of the Virgin never ceased, even though their resonant music in England was quenched for a while ; they were whispered : *Stabat Mater Dolorosa; Regina Cœli, Lætare; Salve, Regina; Alma Redemptoris Mater; Quem terra, pontus, sidera ; O gloriosa Virginum; Memento, rerum Conditor; Ave, Maris Stella; Salve, Mundi Domina ; Salve, Arca fœderis;* and the rest in the " Little Office of the Blessed Virgin Mary." These hymns, in "monkish" Latin, with their singular beauty, break through the recitation of psalms and prayers with the sweetness of rhyme and of metre as the modern ear best understands them, to the scandal of the scholar. These " Hours," as the " Office " is familiarly called, having been for a time the private devotions of the first Christians, were soon made official and public for the whole Church. The first Christians had said "Lauds" at daybreak, and "Vespers" in the evening. The " Matin" service was added, and as the monastic system was established, the monks added " Prime," as a prayer before the day's work ; " Terce," in memory of the descent of the Holy Ghost at that hour ; " Sext " and " Nones " in remembrance of the Apostles' prayers: " Now Peter went to pray about the sixth hour"; "Peter and John went up together into the Temple at the hour of prayer; being the ninth hour." Saint Benedict, the holy father of all western monks, composed " Compline " as the night-prayer of his Order. In due time these monastic " Hours " were in the hands of all who were taught to read. The " Little Office of the Blessed Virgin Mary " is almost entirely made from the Psalms of David. They are ancient, but the hymns are of the great " Dark Ages," and mediæval. Some of the lovely names of them must linger in the memories of English readers by means of Dante. In the *Purgatorio* the rescued souls going to their restoration across the splendid sea, speeding by the

K

wings of the "*uccel divino*," chant the psalm of deliverance, *In exitu Israel de Ægypto*; the souls that had sinned as far as the hour of death, but had in that hour repented and been forgiven, go chanting the penitential psalm *Miserere*; but the hymn *Salve, Regina* is sung among the fragrances and colours of a higher stage by happier spirits. And in Paradise itself is sung the antiphon of the earthly church and cloister, *Regina Cœli, Lætare.*

Although the poetry to be cited in this brief treatise is English poetry, let it be permitted to follow Dante a little longer, for it is hard to leave his company. In the last cantos of the *Paradiso* Saint Bernard, who is in eternal favour with Mary ("Well hast thou written of me, Bernard,") becomes Dante's teacher. "Look," says the Saint, her faithful Bernard, "into the furthermost Circle of Heaven, until thou shalt see, seated, the Queen to whom this Kingdom is subject and devout" ... "I saw," sings Dante, "a thousand rejoicing angels. And there amidst their play and their chanting I saw a Beauty laughing, which was joy in the eyes of all the Saints ... 'Look now into the face that most resembles Christ's, for that splendour shall best make thee ready to look upon Christ' ... So much delight I saw rain upon her ... that nothing, of all I had yet beheld, so amazed me, nor showed me so much of the aspect of God." Then follows the high vision of that "Love" (that Archangel) who went down from Heaven to Mary, and who faces her now in the *Paradiso* with always open wings, singing "Ave," as he looks into her eyes:

> E quell' Amor, che primo lì discese,
> Cantando *Ave, Maria, gratia plena,*
> Dinanzi a lei le sue ali distese.
> Rispose alla divina cantilena
> Da tutte parti la beata Corte.

"Who then is this Angel," asks Dante of Saint Bernard (Saint Bernard "who adorned himself with Mary as the morning star is adorned with the sun ")—"who is this Angel so enamoured that he looks all fire?"

> Ed egli a me: baldezza e leggiadria
> Quant' esser puote in Angelo ed in alma
> Tutta è in lui, e si volem che sia;
> Perch' egli è quegli che portò la palma
> Giuso a Maria, quando 'l Figliuol di Dio
> Carcar si volle della nostra salma.

And soon, close to the place of Mary and close to that of Saint Peter and that of Moses, Dante shows us the seat of Anne, the mother of Mary:

> Tanto contenta di mirar sua figlia,
> Che non muove occhio per cantar Osanna.

It is this passage that Chaucer must have had in mind in this couplet of a prayer in the *Tales*: he is thinking of Paradise—

> That as withouten end is songe Osanne,
> Thou Cristes moder, doughter deere of Anne.

Finally, the great song of the vision of Dante's Paradisal Rose intones its last canto with a prayer of Saint Bernard to the Virgin: "Maiden Mother, daughter of thy Son, more humble and more exalted than any other creature, term of the eternal Counsels, thou art she who hast so ennobled the nature of mankind that the Maker thereof did not abhor to be by it created. In thy womb was love rekindled, and by that warmth, in eternal peace, has grown this Flower. Thou art to us in Paradise the noontide face of charity, and to mortals below thou art the living fountain of hope."

> In te misericordia, in te pietate,
> In te magnificenza, in te s' aduna
> Quantunque in creatura è di bontate.

English readers, moreover, if they have read no further, nor so much as finished the line, have always had by heart the two words of the hymn *Alma Redemptoris*, for the sake of Chaucer's "litel child," the martyr who, with his throat cut by the Jews and their hired "homicyde," still sang this hymn from the "Hours," "fro word to word according with the note." The "litel clergeon, seven years of age," had heard his fellow, a chorister, practising the sacred song, and thereafter gave him no rest until he, too, possessed the notes and the words. Chaucer's infrequent tenderness is evident in his repetitions—"this litel child," "his litel book lerninge," "so yonge and tendre was his age."

> "And is this song maked in reverence
> Of Cristes moder?" seyde this innocent;
> "Now certes I wol do my diligence
> To conne it al, er Cristemasse is went,
> Though that I for my prymer shal be shent
> And shal be beten thryës in an houre."
>
> This litel child, as he cam to and fro
> Ful merily than wolde he singe, and crye
> O Alma Redemptoris ever mo.
>
> This gemme of chastitee, this emeraude,
> And eek of martirdom this ruby bright.
>
> Yet spak this child when spreynd with holy water,
> And song O Alma Redemptoris Mater.
>
> And in a tombe of marbul stones clere
> Enclosen they his litel body swete.

Alma Redemptoris rings throughout the tale, and with such an accent of fondness for little childhood as Chaucer sounds once equally elsewhere, in the passage of Grisildes' trial:

> Have here agen your litel yonge mayde.

VIII. THE ARTS OF COLOUR

SAINT Augustine avers that no portrait of the Blessed Virgin was known to have existed anywhere on earth. Saint Ambrose could find no authority for a description of her person, except as *figura probitatis*, and " clothed with virtues." But at the end of the fourth and the beginning of the fifth centuries legends took shape in the East to the effect that certain images of the Virgin, preserved in Jerusalem, were veritable portraits; by and by they were attributed to the hand of Saint Luke, her Evangelist, so manifestly her friend.

These images were in fact honoured by the Fathers of the Synod of the East, who, on this authority, describe her very colouring: her hair "the colour of ripe corn." In that suburb of Rome, out at the Porta Pia, which was lately a long lonely vineyard, and is now full of thin tall houses and tramcars, the reliquary of the ancient church of Saint Constantia, hard by the Basilica and Catacomb of Saint Agnes, contains a little lock of brown hair which is said to be one cut from that holy head. With these " portraits " and this " relic " begins and ends this wistful attempt to possess some direct record, something other than the conjecture of mere art. But while this dutiful and natural desire for reality lingered doubtfully, having doubtful documents, realism made one sudden grasp at the dear truth, the dear fact. This was on one wall of the Catacombs; and it took place there, underground, before the great art of mosaic, ruling its rigid material by rigid thought, and in turn giving its thought into that rigid and most noble control, put aside for a few centuries the childish and—as it is childish, the filial—desire for a close correspondence with the sacred person and the facts of her personality. The fresco is in the Catacomb of Priscilla, and it shows a real woman clasping a real Child, and the Child is at her breast and clings to it with His hand, turning a startled look over His shoulder. The action is an instinctive action of guarding His own food and sustenance, and resembles that of a young kitten putting its foot on its first plate of food with a little growl of warning. This early-Christian painting has direct relation with Raphael. He who drew this little fresco jumped the symbolic ages, the majestic mosaics. Thirteen centuries before the Madonna della Seggiola, the Suckling of the Catacomb looked round, yes, and with more animation than Raphael's, whose Child has the same young falcon eyes, with their wildness somewhat tamed by the graceful sentiment and decorum of the Renascence.

Professor Adolfo Venturi (to whose knowledge both of art and of tradition my summary pages owe much) takes an Italian view of the sixth-century and eighth-century mosaics when he says, "As decadent art becomes less able to represent thought, we find the figure of Mary despoiled of individuality as of animation, turned into a conventional symbol, the Virgin foretold by Isaiah." This is Italian, perhaps penultimate rather than recent or present Italian, criticism; for even in Italy a newer, and older, spirituality, a spirit different from Raphael's, is assuredly to-day at last awake—if only as part of a fashionable fancy for northern things. It is a tenable opinion that the art of Sant' Apollinare Nuovo at Ravenna, of San Vicenzo at Rome, of San Marco at Florence, of the Duomo at Torcello, of the Martorana at Palermo, and of St. Mark's at Venice—art of the sixth century to the thirteenth —is in all its ages full of growth and life. There are some buds that are difficult to distinguish from pods, and a mosaic of the sixth century may be likened to such a bud. But however this may be judged, one thing should be obvious—that the art which Professor Venturi thinks to have become "less able to represent thought" because it "turns the figure of the Virgin into a conventional symbol," did rather by that act

prove itself " able to represent thought." The fresco in the
Catacomb, on the other hand, represents only the painter's
filial desire for the beloved and precious fact, a desire that
used the faculty of observation vigilantly and well; the designer of this Mary with her eager and jealous suckling had
looked intently and intelligently—surely not necessarily in-
tellectually—at mothers with children at the breast, perhaps
also at little young kittens eating. Intellect, shared among
the three, mother, child, and painter, would not be very
much. And Raphael with his over-praised Madonna shows
himself to be intelligent also, albeit less filial and less desir-
ous for the natural fact than his predecessor in the Dark Ages
and the dark Catacomb; but not necessarily intellectual. He,
on the contrary, who set up the majestic mosaics in those
churches—he who worked in the incomparable spirit of
those great ages, who brought no negligible part of Athens
through Byzantium to Venice and Ravenna, and through
those Adriatic cities to the Mediterranean, and into Roman-
esque and Gothic Italy—he was one who thought. His
symbol, his "convention," was a decision of high and memorable intellect. The word convention, used yesterday as an
insult to art, and used to-day as an insult to morality, resumes
all its dignity in relation to the mosaic art. The artist of
mosaic had a convention with his fellows, with all his fellows;
the thirteenth-century designer agreed not only with his
contemporaries; he respected the best consensus of eight
centuries past, eight centuries that were learning and changing and proving, and increasing in all divine and human
knowledge and in all human dexterity; in spite of change
and development, his work is a sign that the thirteenth century did not despise the sixth. Not for him—whose name
is lost, whose dust, whose ashes, have been the dust and the
ashes of other men many times, not for him, in voluntary
oblivion, was any share of the self-worship that insists upon
the value of this man's view or that man's emotion, or the
other's temperament, and finds in these separations all the

value of human art. Would he have thought it worth while to assure us, like a post-impressionist, of his own sincerity? Not he. He did himself and the world the honour to take his sincerity for granted, and for something that did not need announcing; we do not use the word in regard to him, as we do not praise an honourable woman with the name of her honour.

The mosaic, at its best in the several ages, showing us the maternal figure as something pontifical, transcends the idea of a woman. If the paradox might be permitted, one might say that although a mother is the most womanly of women, this Mother is maternal, not womanly. She passes beyond "womanly," as now and then the greatest poetry passes beyond imagery, even though poetry might (but for those rare and all-cherishable incidents) be defined, itself, as imagery. She is seated with her Child, or she stands without Him, with a saint on either hand in a triumvirate of monition or judgement; and even when she is seated, holding the Infant Christ, she is vested as a priest rather than as a woman. Her Child is her centre, in the midst of her. All, especially in the earlier mosaics, is symmetrical; the august rules of mosaic art in the severest time ruled thus— the usually absolute full face, the two dimensions alone (almost alone, for perspective, though respected, is not displayed), the decorative stillness. Between two arms of her throne she sits erect, an equal angel on either side; her vestments are equal on this side and that, so are her jewels. The Child's smaller nimbus is precisely beneath her larger. He is propped between her two heavily draped knees. The only incidental change of equipoise occurs where one of her hands supports Him, and where He raises His own right hand to give the benediction. Or, even the visible attributes of maternity omitted, Mary stands as the " Orante " of still earlier design, a praying figure, feminine only in the covered head—covered as well as crowned—and in the great burden of jewels; the sacerdotal stole, in San Vicenzo, gives place to shoulder-chains and enormous clasps of gold and stones.

It seems to have been in the beginning of the sixth century that the great dignity of these symbolic and significant images—whether expressed by the majesty of enthronement or by the splendour of coronation—became the general rule of ecclesiastical art. In the latter half of the sixth century Pope Sixtus III (*Sixtus Episcopus Plebi Dei*), the Nestorian heresy overcome and Mary acknowledged Mother of God, decreed the greater ceremonial honour of her image. In Santa Maria Maggiore, in Rome, where some work of a different and less orderly character has recently been brought to light, the finest figure of the Virgin is invested with the pallium and adorned with jewels—the crown about the up-gathered hair, the gem above the brows and in each ear,—seated in a throne furnished with cushion and predella; set in symbols of the faith of the Gentile and the Jew, types, signs, and prophecies.

In all this there was much of the East. But as soon as the West became expert and out of bonds, it was all for the third dimension, for action, for expression, and for drama. When Mary knelt in profile to her Child the age of Mosaic was coming to an end. Thenceforward the agile art of painting comes more and more to life, and mosaic is over. It was a pity it should end in those days, because it was then perfect, and the decoration of a Christian church could do nothing worthier. The figures in the middle dome of Saint Mark's at Venice are so beautiful, so dominant, so eminent in sanctity — without "expression," without emotion—that, as one stands in that shadow, the whole triumph of art still to come seems—unjustly—something like a showy and violent pageant on a downward road. For although, as has been said, the art of mosaic was virtually one art from the sixth century to the thirteenth, it must not be supposed that there had been no progress in it. There was progress, but there was one spirit and one

L

"convention," one obedience to the material and one use of it. In the sixth-century work, the art that was in truth young had something clinging to it that was in decline—an old husk about that bud of life, a last year's autumnal leaf, as in Coleridge's poem, left on the tree in spring. The eyes are too large, the mouth is too small, precisely as they were again in 1830 or thereabout, when Lady Blessington edited " Keepsakes." None the less was the sixth-century art an art of hope, an art that made rules for the great future masters of Saint Mark's.

When I say that the art of mosaic ended there, would it were literally true. The fine art of mosaic ended there, but it was precisely there, in only two or three more centuries, that Italian designers set up in the place of that perfect decoration, much of which they must have torn down, the vulgar mosaics that profane so much of that cathedral. Venice that " held the gorgeous East in fee " in commerce, and was servant and learner of the austere East in art, became Western, Western. And if Venice, how much more the cities further from the East. Mary's mantle by and by flew in a wind of painting and sculpture—nay, in a wind of mosaic, which was a further outrage. But for a time she kept her state. The Cimabue Madonna in Santa Maria Novella—the greatly celebrated—and the Cimabue in the Royal Gallery, the early works of Guido da Siena, Duccio di Buoninsegna, Fra Barnaba da Modena, and Giotto—to name a few masters of that transitory art—retain the mystical Lady of the great Dark Ages. They do not indeed leave her in the place of a judge or high-priest (not high-priestess), of a god (not a goddess), on her inlaid thrones with her rigid child before her; for the painter begins to have a nimble hand, a dramatic thought. But, though the Child begins to be childlike, to look into His Mother's face, soon to talk with her, anon to play with her, Mary is still too grave for expression, too august for movement, except only the benedictory lifting of her Pontifical hand. There is nothing more interesting than the first restlessness, the new Occidental vivacity, not yet out of bonds, of the Madonna and Child of each of these masters, Cimabue perhaps excepted. With the truer human proportions of a child—the larger head—comes inevitably human childishness. The Child in the Bologna Giotto has His arms up, less to embrace His immovable Mother, it seems, than to tease her with grasping at the severe gorget about her chin. Fra Barnaba's Child gives benedictions no more—He is grasping His foot, as a child does. But His Mother does not smile. In the curious picture at Assisi, attributed to Cavallini, there is some close speech between Mother and Child. He turns to her an eager profile, blessing her with the three fingers of a Pope, but evidently blessing her also with animated words; and she with her mouth still silent yet yields to movement—making a gesture, unexplained, with her right hand. The large nimbus and the small intersect each other. The Italians, by the way, have most vital and dramatic hands, but in none of their schools of painting are the hands dramatic. The act and speech of logical reasoning is rendered, even by Leonardo da Vinci, as a counting-off of arguments on the fingers. The cause of this is dark.

Fra Angelico restores for a while the archaic fashion of the small head, the proportions of the adult figure. But expression grave and noble, though explicit, visits, in his frescoes, the eyes of Mary. And among his contemporaries, his successors, expression and movement were not to be stayed again, except in some of the work of the great Mantegna. Mary grows beautiful as other women are beautiful. Her hair is unveiled, soon it is unbound, soon again it is interwoven with subtle textures that do not hide it, and adorned with jewels that are no longer the great stones, breastplates and frontlets of priesthood, but have been set by good Tuscan jewellers. Modern art has its way thenceforward.

Joy enters, tenderness, fear, affliction, ecstasy, triumph, swooning, and tears. "We are symbols, and we inhabit symbols." Therefore it need not be thought that Mary ceases to be symbolic of terrible and heavenly truths because the painter paints her in all facts—the actions of the Gospels, and those related of her childhood, of her education, in all the legends that were believed, and those that were only half believed, in the Middle Ages in all Europe and the nearer East. But ceremonially symbolic, as she had been in the past she ceased to be, in Flanders, Holland, Germany, France, Italy, as the schools increased. And it is greatly consoling, and a high surprise, and if a paradox an important paradox, to find the mystery that had escaped the schools, during what is usually held to be the rise and the culmination of modern art, wonderfully restored in a late school— that of Venice, in the supreme art of Tintoretto. When he, the greatest of the great, entered upon the enterprise of painting, he came into a rich inheritance. Before his day the light of our earthly possession—our sky—had opened on the picture; the third dimension had become—from an intrusion and a slight disturbance—a very treasure to the artist, great riches in a little room, for it had given him an enclosed distance. Venetian colour, the most beautiful thing under the coloured sky, had come to Venice, first in marble, then in the painter's paints. The presentation of emotion, great affliction and tears, had been granted to art when dramatic movement and eloquent eyes and vital gesture had become perfect. But light, distance, tragedy, and colour had not gathered together in mystery until the divine Tintoretto painted a Crucifixion. If the men who first studied the third dimension made one great change in art, he who first turned and looked towards the sun made a change as great, a change singularly glorious. And if Tintoretto was not literally the first who faced the sun, he was surely the first who had such eagle eyes. With the magnificent light came the magnificent shadow; with the shadow and the light, magnificent mystery. It is a mournful and a wounding thing to hear painters of our own fleeting day praised for mystery because they can paint—and we thank them, and admire their sight and their skill—the beauty of mist or even of fog. This is not mystery, and the noble word should not so be used. Mystery of shadow under the sky, and of light (and that of light the more mysterious), and mystery of colour, which the painter of mere mist forgoes or almost forgoes, these are the mystery perceived and honoured by Tintoretto. And we perceive, with him, with what human dignity the head is invested which he contemplates against the light, casting its own shadow on its own noble shoulders and breast.

But this is too much about "art," the thing which always tempts the modern man and woman, however temperate and economical in regard to other matters of discourse, to speak or write too many words. It is more to the point of this little treatise to contemplate the group of women at the foot of Tintoretto's divine Crucifix and of the eternal Passion; and the Mother pierced through with the grief foretold—the great figure of broken-hearted maternity, the symbol of the eternal Compassion—fainting in their gentle arms.

IX. MODERNISM

AND yet a few more words about art must be written, because the history of the devotion to Mary has been the history of the Arts.

Modern art began—art began to be modern—many centuries ago, and went on its restless way; but art was modern as never before in our own time—modern in a new and final manner—when it turned to retrace its steps, when it tried to see with bygone eyes long blind, to feel with bygone hearts long still, and to understand with minds perplexed no more. Thus it is surely true that the smooth and pretty things painted by Bouguereau—albeit all too new—were not so modern as a " Carpenter's Shop " by Millais of much the same epoch, for in the English work there was a conscious interruption of the march of things. We may not love Bouguereau (we make free with his name because it represents a certain date in France), but Bouguereau was in order. He was a continuation, and an effect, and the past through all its movement had steadily led up to him. He was entirely legitimate, and in the line of progress. Corruption too is in the march of things. The better pictures of the pre-Raphaelites, on the other hand, were modern, most modern, because modernism had, as it were, come to a pause, and had turned back: whither? The decision was arbitrary; and thus the march was no longer orderly. The choice proved the excellence of the modern taste, it is true, for the choice reached beyond and behind Raphael, and tried to recover the youth and the singleness of heart of the centuries when art youthfully loved its own advance and was in haste to grow up. But there are two pictures by the chiefs of this English movement in which the fancy

78

is assuredly rather ingenious than imaginative; and of an ingenuity wholly modern. Both invent retrospectively a prophecy of the Passion of Our Saviour, and the invention is not an act of valuable imagination. In Millais' picture the Boy, in His foster-father's workshop, has wounded the little hand that is later to grow ready for the nail of crucifixion. In Holman Hunt's "Shadow of the Cross," an accidental shadow of the body of Christ, stretching weary arms at the close of a day's work, accidentally combines with the horizontal line of a row of tools to form a cross. Is this worthy to be called imagination? Is not the phantasy of very little cost?

Rossetti, on the other hand, had a better judgement. His design, "The Passover," is symbolical in a better way. Here is no cheap fancy or invention of paltry accidents. Rossetti has painted an actual incident of a Paschal Day at Nazareth (the incident itself the symbol) and has drawn it as a simple and forthright record of a greatly significant fact. He shows the keeping of the Passover during the boyhood of Christ, and Christ Himself bringing the sacrificial blood of the lamb which was a prophecy of His own. Here is no play with a wounded hand or the chance shadow of a cross. Rossetti himself, in a letter to Coventry Patmore, describes the subject of his work as an incident

which must have actually occurred during every year of the life led by the Holy Family . . . the one Sacrifice really typical of the other. In this respect . . . I think you will acknowledge it differs entirely from Millais', or any other of the very many which resemble it in so far as they are illustrations of Christ's life "subject to His parents," but not one of which that I can remember is anything more than an entire and often trifling fancy of the painter, in which the symbolism is not really inherent in the fact, but merely suggested or suggestible, and having had the fact made to fit it.

If Rossetti had not here written his meaning in the unpremeditated words of a letter, he might have stated it in better form, but it is an admirable meaning. The "destroyer of all heresies" seems to have kept her poet of the "Ave" on the right road of art.

Her direction has never been invoked, or has been with-drawn, in the cases of the painters of "Christ in the House of His Parents," and "The Shadow of the Cross." The difference between these two "religious" paintings and those of the veritable times before Raphael is to be found not only in the little trick of ingenuity, but even more manifestly in the neglect of the dignity of Mary. This is to be seen less in Millais' picture; though here too Mary, binding her Son's hand, is but a faded housewife, and the model was told to look as though she had a headache. But in Holman Hunt's, the little shuffling figure kneeling at her box of treasures, and the insignificant head, are signs not of her presence in this post-vaticinatory scene, but of her absence from the painter's heart and art. Other things he possesses, besides his power as a painter—a good will, sin-cere intention, and faith in his own work—but the sanction which the "Madonna" bestowed upon the painting of the schools of the past, the benediction that she bestows with a Pontiff's gesture from the apse of the Byzantine Cathedral, is not there.

This undeniable failure of two pictures, works of a time (not long gone by) of enthusiasm in England, recalls the suggestion of one of the titles of honour offered to the Virgin—"who alone hast overcome all heresies." She was held to be the touchstone of orthodoxy. And she is here the touchstone of religious art; she has manifestly defeated the heretics of art—not these two modern men and their like, their contemporaries, only. She personally administers the ordeal to the painters named a moment ago, but she administered the same, though to a different effect, to the painters of the decadence after Raphael. A very few bore the test.

We have to-day other heresies than those of Nestorius and Arius, whose errors were put to the touch by the doctrine standing around her person, the doctrine of herself. The modern world has brought forth many heresies, but two chiefly must be named because of their portent and importance: one, the assertion of the pride of life at the time of the Renascence; and one, the denial of compassion by the philosophy of to-day—or is it already of yesterday? The doctrine that stands around the person of the Virgin Mother attributes to her absolute humility in confessed and conscious dependence upon a superhuman good; and the same doctrine attributes to her an entire and immeasurable Compassion, a Compassion facing and reflecting the Passion of Christ. To those two heresies, therefore, the pride of life and the denial of compassion, she administers proof and reproof, her own manner of ordeal and her own word of condemnation, signally and in perfection.

Nor less certain is it that she—the doctrine of herself—administered an ordeal to the whole civilization rising in Europe after the decay and destruction of Antiquity. She administered it there, and humility was at once honoured; often outraged, never denied. Compassion, by the same test, was at once enshrined, beloved; also often outraged, never denied.

X. IN CHURCHES

THE image of the Virgin Mary in art underwent the changes, the progress, the triumph, and the downfall more conspicuously, more exemplarily, than, for instance, the image of the Crucifixion. The Crucifix could not undergo much evil from the cleverness of the most successful sculptor or painter, though indeed there have been "Depositions from the Cross," in which the later painters enjoyed their own composition, drama, and muscular action to their heart's desire; and the worst Raphael in the world—the "Entombment" in the Borghese Gallery—makes all profit from the occasion, and most heartlessly. But throughout the schools of all times and nations the Crucifixion must needs be simple, nearly symmetrical, as the outward shape of man is symmetrical, and rigid with the motionless attitude of the Cross.

Far from simple, unluckily, need be the "Assumption." The painters who flourished—the word is every way appropriate—in the later and lower stages of Italian art loved a flourishing "Assumption." The judicious admirer values Titian's great picture chiefly for the tender half-shadows, shadows with light in them, on the under-parts of the flying cherubim, and not for the drama of the rushing figure mounting skywards in its coloured garments. The "Coronation" has no such opportunities of movement, and thus the later artists generally leave it to the gentle Primitives. But with the flowing and flying "Assumption" the sculpture as well as the painting of the decadence was eagerly busy. At Chartres when, in A.D. 1763, they had torn down the beautiful carved screen of the thirteenth century they no doubt found the sculpture as well as the

architecture too little flourishing, and over the high altar
they made, two years later, a flutter of clouds, and a soaring
Mary whose girdle swings scroll-wise to the wind, in the
manner then accustomed. It is not altogether to be re-
gretted that art, passing through inevitable phases, should
have set up here its own defiant and triumphant altar-piece.
The age that produced it was the last age that believed
simply in itself. It is not that age, but the age following,
that confuses history. For the ages following have not
believed in themselves, and they are, as has been said in a
former page, in a deeper and more significant sense modern.
Confusing history in their own time, and yet studying it
humbly for its past, modern men dodge about the many
ages seeking styles (and finding none) and seeking them so
restlessly that the time is not far off when the style of the
sculptor of the "Assumption," with the curl of his cloud
and ribbon at the head of the upright nave and choir of
Chartres, will be resumed, re-chosen, re-admired. Already
we hear the first resumption of the praises of Bernini,
whereas it is but half a score of years ago that Bernini's
name was a name of reproach and hissing. It is, no doubt,
time that we should acknowledge that master's dominant
success, the spirit of his gesture, the glory of his flourish,
the royalty of his attitude; but an even fuller tolerance of his
style is coming now upon us in its inevitable turn; so bent
are we upon that very turn, the turn back that pauses, at
choice, upon all periods—the later yesterday, the earlier to-
day, or, in the contrary sense, pounces now upon the Primitives and anon upon the eighteenth century, and will soon
alight upon something midway.

Yet Chartres itself might have ruled over connoisseurship
to better order. The architectural sculptures of Chartres
are a great example of the steady march from one stage of
fine and incorrupt art to another, with dignity in every
change. These sculptures begin with the twelfth century
and pass through the perfection of the thirteenth. The

twelfth-century Virgin and Child of the west front is the perfectly symmetrical full-faced Mother, and the symmetrical Child, such as we know them throughout the great mosaics; but the change of a brief century, or somewhat less, brings us to more energetic symbolism, such as that of Mary standing upon the conquered evil; to the two delicately dramatic feminine figures of the Visitation, with natural drapery, speaking faces; to the action of the Epiphany, and Mary seated in three-quarters. And the changes of five centuries carry us to the completion and finality of developed sculpture. The sixteenth-century work of Jehan Soules, in its place and age, it would be difficult to praise too highly; nor would any but a rigid lover of the early art for the sake of its date refuse admiration to the beautiful seventeenth-century work of Jean de Dieu d'Arles. Over all these necessary changes presides alike the figure of Mary.

Chartres is unique for the system of its sculptural architecture, but throughout all the great cathedrals of France runs the same history; and in England, where the image, as Wordsworth says, has fallen, the Lady Chapel keeps— though it keeps nothing else—its name; an unnecessary corner, an unexplained nook, with architecture standing, as it were, about some centre that is gone. But if great art waxed and waned in its service to the history and the legend of the Blessed Virgin, what has our little day been about— our modern day? Not "modern" in the now venerable sense that refers to the re-civilization of Europe after the fall of Rome; nor "modern" in the later sense which we use to denote the beginning of the Christian arts in the early Middle Ages; nor "modern" as the description of the general decadence of painting after the day of the greatest Venetians; but the new and present "modern" of our own brief day.

The picture-gallery—more rightly the exhibition—yields us little or nothing. A little maternity is there, and a little maidenhood, on its way to marriage, but seldom the entire Virgin Mary; or what is now and then attempted is perhaps "for art's sake." He that saveth his art shall lose it. But in regard to the art of sculpture, the exhibitions have virtually abandoned the Virgin and Child, the group by the Cross, and the Pietà. Mr. Sargent's work in the Boston Library—the work of a great sculptor very suddenly revealed—is a surprise of the time and stands alone. But in regard to the art of the churches, in which popular pleasure, popular devotion, and popular admiration—all important matters, not to be dismissed with irony—set up their images of Virginity and Maternity, we have to review a general continental toy-shop. Whether from the church workshops of Paris and Brussels or from the somewhat more educated one of Munich, the doll is with us, in our travels, introduced, on side-altars, into the very presence of the pontifical Virgin of the mosaics, or the grave Madonna of Tuscany, or the emotional Madonna of Rome, or the many thousand Virgins from Flanders to Spain.

There is a word that seems to denote the decline from dignity of all the images of the later schools; it is that unlucky word "grace"; and the dancing-master in Alfred de Musset's play, who enjoins upon his pupil that when she is dancing to the right she must turn her head to the left, and who skims the stage to show her how expertly it is to be done, is a right Raphaelite. The Raphaelite School would even exact from him and his class as many as three graceful contradictions; the head this way and the shoulders another, and the hips again in a various direction,—but that human nature cannot easily accomplish so much; the painters had the unfair conditions and privileges of paint, and the painted figure cannot fall down. When a French tongue ascribes "grace" to a woman, we hear the word with a vague distaste. Now the really popular Madonna in the churches—a Madonna below any kind of art—is a doll, but a doll less elaborately jointed than the figure of Raphaelite painting;

indeed not jointed at all. It, at least, is not "graceful"; a rigid cheap doll whose form is clearly intended to be much dressed in order to conceal its imperfections. It might hardly be too fantastic to see, in this little puppet stiffly clad and hung with ornaments, as it stands in the wayside places within the churches of Italy, not always advanced to the dignity of altars, but set up in improvised places of honour against pillars or near the doors—to see in this image something of the ancient gravity. Something more of it is here, assuredly, than in the corrupt following of Raphael, if only because the small dressed Madonna-doll is not jointed, having cost the town little money, though it has gained from the citizens many prayers to the Madonna invisible. More like to the twelfth-century sculpture of Chartres, let us dare to say, is this poor doll with a crown than the flying figure of the Assumption in the taste of the late Renascence. The villagers' image wears real ribbons, and the ribbons of the rising, cloud-sustained seventeenth-century Virgin are of marble. Of the two image-makers it is not certain that the able sculptor has the best of it. But the tourist is naturally shocked by the poor puppet in the churches of his tour, and the villagers would doubtless have a jointed doll if they could afford one. So did Giotto improve upon Cimabue by giving posture to his figures, and Raphael was minded greatly to improve upon Giotto.

XI. THE EFFECTUAL INFLUENCE

WITH unparalleled unanimity a long line of centuries secured the place of a Woman and a Child as paramount in the second European civilization. For seven centuries the new arts never wearied of these central figures—the Virgin and Child, the Holy Family, the Virgin and Child and the boy Saint John, the Virgin and her mother, Saint Anne, and her Child. Greek art surviving in Byzantium, Roman art surviving in Central Italy, Lombard art beginning in North Italy, Gothic art through the whole group of transalpine countries—Flanders, Holland, Germany, France, and England—the art of aged and of fresh energies—all alike gave the highest place to this image of Innocence.

Mankind has carefully counted its sufferings caused by religion: so much of controversial and sectarian wars, persecutions, superstitions, and the cruel terrors of consciences: the sum is great. But who has numbered the mercies, the pardons, the generosities, the devoted souls, the bodies self-sacrificed, the weak defended, the young respected, the child fostered, the boy kept incorrupt, the maid sheltered, the lady worshipped, the harlot pitied, the foundling gathered up, the innocent Saint lurking secure in the turbulent families—Borgia, Pazzi, Sforza? And these are only the direct bestowals of the Woman and Child. Outside of that immediate effect of their presence are all the enormous charities and alms of Christendom—the hospital, the ambulance, the monastic feeding of the poor, the Geneva convention, the school, the old-age pension—works, as it were, of the adult Christ.

The doctor of theology is not a sentimentalist; there are

other things than pity to be reckoned with in religion. Nay, there are no thinkers, no manner of teachers, who less merit that name, just now of easy scorn; but even the theologian, before the perpetual image, is known to talk the theological equivalent to "the little language"—the perpetual image of a little woman and a little child. Without the central compassion for the two weak creatures, woman and child, Mary and her Infant, this wicked world would have been incalculably more wicked. Woman and Child have been often oppressed ; what would then have been the oppression? And man is born to fears, and religious fear is the overwhelming fear. But the Virgin and Child stand not for fear, not for death, but for happy life; nor for judgement, but for tenderness. Let it be added that images were read for many ages, day by day, by the bookless. The beneficence of the image of the Virgin and Child can hardly be appraised by us who can read print: the unquestioned, the undoubted Innocence, the central Simplicity. Century by century Europe cherished at its heart the image—whether rude or beautiful, whether the mere searching for a form, or the accomplished modelling or painting by the expert— of these two weak things. All sorts and conditions of men turned in homage to the two helpless persons of the human race. Even when the Byzantine and early Italian Virgin was figured rigid in her hierarchic enthronement, it was known that her innocence and her simplicity had placed her there, and had set the young Child upon her magnificent knees. No other two, in the history of human art, have so nourished the sense of generosity and of forbearance in the adult and manly heart of mankind.

Architecture, Painting, and Sculpture had begun to decline when Literature was making way among the lay populations. Literature, now universal in Europe, once comprised virtually in a little " Book of Hours," has undertaken the ancient devotion in its own form. For our time and nation, the image of the Virgin and Child is entrusted to Coventry Patmore's poem, the image of the Mother most Sorrowful is given into Dante Gabriel Rossetti's, the picture of the Assumption is translated into Francis Thompson's. There we leave them in no less beauty and dignity of custody than when the prophecies were interpreted in the Cloister: " My root is in an honourable people, and in the portion of my God His inheritance, and my abode is in the full assembly of the Saints"; "I am the Mother of fair love and of holy hope"; "Who is she that looketh forth as the morning, fair as the moon, clear as the sun, terrible as an army with banners?" and finally, " Who is she that cometh up from the wilderness, flowing with delights, leaning on her Beloved?"

But the most significant, and the least considered, of all the prophecies is the first, spoken by no prophet but by the mouth of the Creator in the allegory of Eden; the woman was there appointed and announced the opponent of moral evil, as one woman, " our tainted nature's solitary boast," in Wordsworth's phrase, was to overcome it. But it was of woman in all ages, and not only of that victrix, that the Father said to the mystical representative of moral evil upon earth, "I will put enmity between thee and the woman."

> Not she with traitorous kiss her Saviour stung,
> Not she denied Him with unholy tongue.
> She, while Apostles shrank, could danger brave,
> Last at the Cross and earliest at the Grave.

THE END